MW00935046

TwM

Personal Development Guide for Women

Book 1

By Maria Henderson

"Truly, the greatest gift you have to give is that of your own self-transformation."

-Lao Tzu

Introduction

~

There is a world, where you have it all.

A place where you possess inner strength, self-awareness and an unwavering sense of self confidence. Where peace and harmony is more common than that of a chaotic household, a disorganized life and an unstable inner emotional world, where screaming at your children, an unhappy partner and feeling crappy is normal.

Instead, there is a fresh bouquet of beautifully bloomed in-season flowers on your countertop, as you serve a nutritious filled breakfast to your well-behaved children, while pouring a cup of perfectly brewed coffee to your partner whom absolutely adores you.

The morning sun is beaming through your kitchen window and it's another beautiful day, where all is harmonious, you are doing your passion, raising your children in perfect harmony, loving your marriage and life makes complete sense, you are where you're meant to be, and everything is everything.

Sound impossible?

There are many women whom want it all, as I am one of them. Whom want a thriving career, to make a killing; financially, to have a thriving, happy and healthy family, and a passionate filled marriage. But can't handle the challenges and the delicate balance required to managing it all, or worst… may not even know how to.

The simple act of *wanting* without action doesn't get anyone results and doing the same things with expecting different results, calls for insanity. You could say, that I am writing this for me and for all the women whom are in search for a mindful approach to balancing Motherhood and everything else. A new mindset causes action and can bring new results in your life. It's the matter of figuring out your way and what I've found is The Boss Mom Mentality.

My journey of Motherhood has had a profound impact on the woman I am today. Years ago, I was not ready to be responsible for raising another *being*. Nonetheless, with the decisions I've made along the way, I was thrusted into the life of Motherhood, whether I wanted it or not and I had a decision to make.

Do I let Motherhood happen to me?

Or do I take Motherhood into my own hands?

After some very challenging moments in this new chapter, I decided to do the latter. Now as a Mom, I owe it to my girls, to be grounded and thoughtful, to know that every decision I make hereon, affects them. I wrote this book, for my personal healing and to connect to my most authentic self and sharing this with you.

I have had as obsession for Personal Development, cognitive behavior, science of the brain, and how emotions play a huge role in the day to day decision making process for many people. I tend to be impulsive, seeking approval from others, desperately wanting to be enough and ultimately resulting in having a very tumultuous inner emotional world. I needed to be different, better, healthier… inside.

After my very personal in-depth analysis and research for the past fifteen years, I've gathered information and research by psychologist, therapist, psychiatrists and thought leaders throughout the world and across the span of time, that make The Boss Mom Mentality.

Harmoniously applying these Principles and Core Values, can create changed behavior, successful and a meaningful life, filled with fulfilling relationships and a deeper connection with yourself.

Be Open Minded

~

"Let your love propel your beloved into the world and into the full experience of who they are. In this will you have truly loved."

-Neal Donald Walsch, An uncommon Dialogue Conversations with God.

The Boss Mom Mentality is a motivating and fun way to learn about yourself, to become impactful, possess the ability to lead in a mindful way and to become the positive role model for your children and those of your community.

Being open minded while you take the journey of The Boss Mom Mentality will allow you to uncover your personal power, develop your self-awareness through Personal Development and raising your children on your own terms with your own traditions and values. Self-Awareness is the bedrock to this journey, be open to what arises for you.

If you enter this journey of Motherhood with a mindset of, *what can I learn from in these moments?*

Then, a pivotal and very important mental shift can take place within, where growth into your womanhood and cultivating your Boss Mom Mentality is possible.

This is exactly what I needed to do & am still growing into. I encourage you to take the same powerful mental shift and ask yourself these very meaningful questions:

What can I learn from in these moments of Motherhood?

How do I access my inner Boss Mom?

The Boss Mom Mentality is broken up into three sections, each comprised of Principles, weaved together by Core Values. The sections are broken up into phases that moms would enter into starting their journey of mom-life.

Section One; Myths of Motherhood is about overcoming the unknown, relinquishing the opinions of others, fear of failure and the myths of Motherhood.

Section Two; Personal Development & Digging Deep is about understanding who we need to become through Personal Development for our children, families and most importantly for ourselves.

Section Three; Inner Peace & Balance, which is all about maintaining our sanity, cultivating our inner peace and managing time wisely.

Cultivating daily habits towards developing strong characteristics that embody The Boss Mom

Mentality is the goal… as Stephen Covey says, "*we become what we repeatedly do.*"

There is power in knowing your inner strength, your capabilities, a strong sense of self-awareness and creating habits that support your Motherhood journey. I hope that the following pages evoke a level of inspiration, growth and bringing forth the Boss Mom that lives in each and every one of you!

"Every day and in every way, I am getting better and better."

-Emile Coue

Don't Talk About It, Be About It!

~

"He who wishes to secure the good of others has already secured his own."

-Confucius

We would all like to think that we have it all together and things are moving and grooving. Unfortunately, most of us aren't well aware of our downfalls and aspects of ourselves that we can improve on so that we can actually call ourselves Boss Moms and be that person for our families. Falsely claiming to be on your shit, while not putting the work in, to truly being that, seems to plague our society.

What does a Boss Mom really look like, who are they and what do they stand for?

Let us review the meaning of what a Boss Mom is, how it relates to Personal Development and clarify the characteristics of a Boss Mom. There are different interpretations of what a Boss Mom is.

Within the pages ahead, I am referring to a woman whom is a Boss in her life, not professionally speaking, but within an emotional and mental capacity. A level of maturity a woman embodies that takes charge of her personal power, knows her value, understands who she is and utilizes her strengths to accomplish her goals, while developing her weaknesses to be more impactful.

Thus, a Boss Mom possesses a sense of authentic self confidence that comes from within and not defined by her title at work, what her career status is, the car she drives or home she owns… her self confidence comes from a place within, which can't be taken away from her no matter the ups or downs of her life.

The Boss Mom Mentality is a way of *being*, a mentality that a woman embodies or develops throughout her journey of Motherhood. An unwavering belief, which stands in power, truth, love and grace.

Are you a Boss Mom in your life?

Myths of Motherhood

- Learn to Work Through the Emotional Rollercoaster
- Challenges to Prepare for
- Value of Unbalance
- Realistic Sense of Reality
- The Gift

Section One

~

Myths of Motherhood

"There is only one corner of the universe you can be certain of improving... and that's your own self."

-Aldous Huxley

The Boss Mom embodies a woman's journey in taking control of her chapter in Motherhood, uncovering her personal power and standing in her strength while raising her children and managing a busy life.

Section One uncovers the beginning stages of Motherhood; the myths that may be portrayed by society and social media, uncovering a realistic side to Motherhood and what to mentally and emotionally prepare for.

I find that anytime I am mentally prepared for something, I can handle the actual process and outcome better. It's the concept of priming your brain that I will review in length within this book and developing a mental state of positive outcomes that help you through this new journey.

The Boss Mom Mentality is exactly that, a woman that mentally prepares for situations to ensure positive and beneficial outcomes.

Characteristics of a Boss Mom

Become a Boss Mom

Self Aware
Confident
Fair
Fierce
Diplomatic
Patient
Rational
Determined
Dependable
Honest
Committed
Brave
Optimistic
Resilient

NOTES:

- Principle 1 -

Learn to Work Through the Emotional Rollercoaster

Principle 1

~

Work Through the Emotional Rollercoaster

"Conflicts create the fire of affects and emotions; and like every fire it has two aspects: that of burning and that of giving light."

-Dr. Carl Jung

I was not ready for Motherhood. When I had discovered that I was expecting, I was 28 years old and had barely made a year anniversary with my live-in boyfriend. Nonetheless, we were thrilled to be parents, he more than I…I was terrified to take on this responsibility. Somewhere inside, I felt unworthy of being a mom to something so precious.

During these moments, my insecurities were screaming louder than ever.
"I am not ready for this, who am I to be a mom to a little baby…"
"What if I f*ck up!?"
"What if I can't afford it?
"What if my boyfriend leaves me?"

Everything under the sun of worrying came over me for the first couple of days. However, after those voices subsided, I was left with myself… lying in bed, wondering…
"How does my baby look like?"
"What would she feel like in my arms?"
"How would it be like to have a family of my own?"

I don't know what came over me, but I felt a warm sensation within my heart and a feeling that I could do it… somehow, someway, I would do it and that everything was going to be fine. I was a smoker at the time, so I immediately gave up smoking. Somehow, when I made that emotional connection to Motherhood, my mentality also shifted, my brain switched, and I immediately saw cigarettes as poison to my unborn child. Was this the start to becoming a responsible mother? Perhaps… but I still needed much growing to do.

When I had my daughter, my partner had to start traveling for work. We were devastated to found out that we would only have two weeks together with our new child and that he was going to be gone for three weeks at a time… three weeks away, one-week home and this went on for two and a half years. These moments were the loneliest times for me, as a new mom facing new responsibilities.

Those closest to me played their typical mind games that seemed more obvious now that I was responsible for a baby, which caused a rift. Visits and phone calls became far and few between & eventually stopped altogether. This was tough to deal with and feelings of unhealed emotions arouse from childhood. Just my luck, dealing with my own emotional baggage while raising a brand-new baby all by myself, so it felt.

To make things worse, friends fell off, as we all were going through different changes and entering into different chapters of our lives. I was very lonely, and I didn't know how to deal with these new feelings. I was experiencing bouts of emotional ups and downs and I had diagnosed myself with having a mild case of post-partum depression… thanks to web md.

At this point I'd realized that having a child was going to force me to deal with my own emotional unhealed wounds, otherwise it was going to eat me alive. This is the moment in my journey where I needed to do something different than stew in my negative emotions and blaming other people for my emotional instability and unhappiness. I knew that actions create change, creating new results and choosing something different than that of my past.

Don't let the emotional rollercoaster rule your Motherhood journey, your future or any subsequent chapters of your life. Let's review some actionable tips that can help with working on strengthening your inner world and learn some ways to work through your emotions.

Talk to a Therapist

~

Even if you feel like you are fine, seek help. In the midst of being the main caregiver of my newborn, the thought of me suffering from Postpartum Depression seemed unlikely. I felt that it only counted for extreme cases like wanting to kill myself or harm my baby and that was not the case in my situation. I love my daughter and enjoyed all of our amazing moments together...but I still felt bouts of unhappiness, loneliness, questioning my relationships around me, sadness and depression.

Just because you might not experience the intense feelings that come with suicidal thoughts, that doesn't mean you shouldn't seek professional help. You should talk to someone if you are feeling any level of emotional instability. Become honest and vulnerable enough to allow yourself to heal through these moments by opening up to someone you can trust. These are the moments where you can honestly reveal and release the tensions that plague your mind.

Don't Rely on Your Partner

~

Talking to a Therapist allows you to work through your emotions and can walk you through a more rational point of view of your current situation. A big mistake that I made was relying on my partner to walk me through my feelings and expecting him to give me emotional support or uplift me.

Like mine, your partner probably isn't a professional. They don't have the training or objectivity to help guide you through the tough times while they themselves are invested in you and your baby's well-being. In fact, that will stress them out causing a bigger issue within the relationship. Don't put that expectation on them. Seek professional help.

It might be hard to admit that you are struggling, but it is harder to struggle alone. You aren't a bad mom if you have postpartum depression or are emotionally unstable. There is power in communicating your feelings and seeking help makes you stronger. Allow yourself to be vulnerable enough to heal… this is what helped me. Being able to let out my frustrations to a professional, so I could work through them gave me a rational approach to my irrational thought process.

Explore with Your Baby

~

Explore the world with your little one! Go grocery shopping, visit friends and family, go to the park, take walks, get some sunshine, get out of the house! I didn't do much of this my first year, I was in such a terrible mindset that even getting out of the house was a stressful experience.

I feared the unknown, what happens if she shits herself in the car and we are on the highway? What if I get a flat tire and we're in the middle of the road and I have no one to help me?

I was a mess... thinking the worst which ended up paralyzing me. The lesson here is to explore, get used to being out with your little one, practice getting in and out of the car seat, multitasking and developing self-confidence of being a mom. Taking your mind off of your household, out of those four walls and being out and about can definitely change your mood and creates for overall happier moments. Don't be afraid to go out and enjoy it!

Make Mom Friends

~

A huge mistake that I made early on in my mom-hood, is that I isolated myself due to my negative mindset. This perpetuated negative outcomes and didn't help me get out of the debilitating thought process. Now that I have experienced this in my own life, I encourage all moms to do the opposite. Having friends who are going through the same things as you are create more of a comfortability and openness about what you are going through. Invoking a Boss Mom Mentality is creating a support system with likeminded people, in this case, like minded mommas!

Making mom friends is a great resource to allow some *wooosah* moments, share some laughter and allows your baby to interact with other babies. I suggest Googling Mom Groups within your community, Mom Runs or Mom Walks, or Toddler Reads at a local library or rec center. Facebook has several local mom groups.

Reach out! There are new moms everywhere and you can bet that they're looking for mom friends, too.

Enjoy Every Moment

~

You know well enough that the days, weeks and months will always be different as your little one grow up. One week we are dealing with sleep regression, the next we are dealing with a tooth coming in, the next they are crawling, then walking. The days (and the nights when they just won't sleep!) seem so long but the weeks and months and years seem to fly by too quickly.

You won't cherish the blowout diapers or supermarket tantrums in the moment and that's okay. One day you'll look back and wish they were so little again. I know I do!

Read, Watch & Learn

~

Other Personal Development and Self-Help books that I have accumulated in the past decade was ultimately the profound encouragement of writing this book. My best friends, encouraged me, inspired me and motivated me to keep moving forward, everyone from Dr. Wayne Dyer, Deepak Chopra, Brene Brown, Napoleon Hill and Robert Collier, to name a few. These many books provided enlightenment during my journey of confusion and loneliness.

Feed your mind with encouragement, listen to positive music, lectures or shows. What you feed your mind, creates a ripple effect in how you perceive your current situation, creates action and dictate your results. Become open to the little inspiration of the art around you, whether they come in a form of textbooks, shows, people, music etc. They all provide some sort of inspiration.

Conclusion

~

Emotional Rollercoasters during Motherhood is normal, it's the way we go about handling them that makes all the difference. I worried too much; I was going through bouts of emotions and I didn't know how to deal with them all.

What helped me to understand my crazy emotions was talking to a Professional, seek help even when you don't think you need it. We all need help and support at every stage of our lives and definitely at the beginning of Motherhood more than any other, when hormones are high, and we are adjusting to a new role in our lives.It will help you understand that the feelings you have are normal and will eventually subside. Stay positive and talk to people, get yourself out of the house, be interactive and explore.

The good news is that all of these negative feelings have subsided for me and eventually will for you, too. Congrats on becoming a Mother and the start of your exciting journey.

NOTES:

~ The Boss Mom Community ~

Arista Ilona

"Motherhood isn't about perfection, it's a catalyst to a spiritual transformation, a personal journey that will inspire you to emerge."

The Boss Mom Mentality

- Principle 2 -

Challenges to Prepare For

Principle 2

~

Challenges to Prepare For

"By failing to prepare, you are preparing to fail."

-Benjamin Franklin

In light of preparation for Motherhood, it's a chapter in life where one learns most through experience. You can read all the books, finish this book from cover to cover and go to all the seminars, or watch all the How-To videos, but nothing prepares you for the moment your doctor hands your tiny miracle to you and life happens.

Some say the birth is the easiest part. Everything that comes after, is going to force you to stretch, grow out of your comfort zone and transform you into the woman you were meant to be, if you are open to it. Embracing this amazing challenge is a blessing that one could only be so honored to take on.

Here are four common challenges New Moms face, like myself and tips on how to approach Motherhood as smoothly as you can possibly allow.

Your Needs Come Last

~

All of your focus and energy will be on your newborn for the first few months. You might forget to eat, walk the dog, or take a shower. That's all understandable and part of the deal, but, probably sooner than you think, you'll have to think about yourself again. At least a little bit.

You can't pour from an empty cup.

The Boss Mom Mentality is about being honest enough to ask for help. Call your mother, let your husband step in so you can shower, or find a babysitter so you can run to the store alone. Your baby is your priority, but make sure you're a priority to yourself, too. It can be hard when your career was your priority and it's been replaced with your baby. Or it can be tough on your partner when all of your focus is on the baby and it feels like they've been pushed to the side.

It happens to everyone. The most important thing to know is that attention shifts and refocused and everything balances out, eventually. For now, your focus should be on you and your baby. Everything will even out again, soon.

Lack of Sleep

~

My first child was tough, she cried every night, when she finally settled into a sleeping schedule, it was short lived. We'd suffered from sleep regression, and the pattern went on. My eldest hadn't slept straight through the night consistently until she turned a year old. I was luckier with my second child, but my first child had braced us to be prepared for some rough nights ahead.

Prepare yourself for this, your little one wont sleep as much as you would like. When you're in the middle of a pre-dawn feeding and getting into bed just as soon as your husband's alarm clock goes off, you'll wonder how you can continue existing with such little sleep.

This moment in your baby's time last for only that moment in their life. It might be tomorrow night, or it might be the next day or week, but your baby will sleep and, eventually, you will too. One day you'll look back and wonder how on earth you did it.

If you're a coffee drinker, ask for coffee shop gift cards for your birthday or Christmas. If you aren't, treat yourself to good pillows and sheets. The lack of sleep isn't easy, but it'll make the sleep you do get (and the coffee you drink when you don't) so much sweeter.

Unsolicited Advice

~

Don't you hate the advice you've already gotten about your baby and how to raise her? Everyone seems to have all the answers, while their results are a joke.
Maybe your sister-in-law has been bugging you for the last few months or your coworker have been giving you "helpful hints" every few hours at work. Once your baby is in your arms or in your stroller or car seat, it seems like everyone you pass on the street or in the grocery store has an opinion on how your baby should be dressed, fed or carried.

It's irritating, you are a grown woman and you're responsible for your baby. No one can make you do anything. As long as your baby is safe and healthy, you do what you need to do.

Conclusion

~

"Every adversity, every failure, every heartache carries with it the seed of an equal or greater benefit."

-Napoleon Hill, Think and Grow Rich

Preparing for anything takes strategic tactfulness and we can only prepare for Motherhood the best way we can… but most lessons will be learned through the thick of it, through the sleepless nights, through the crying fests and through the extremes of your hormonal imbalance.

We can, however, mentally prepare yourself for those moments, journal about it, talk to other moms going through it, anything to help with understanding this new chapter will help you. We don't grow if we aren't challenged and Motherhood is a challenging but richly rewarding time for growth in your womanhood and development.

Embrace the tough times, only then is your character and your personal capabilities strengthen and the easy moments will be a walk in the park.

NOTES:

~ The Boss Mom Community ~

Vanessa Chika Nzeh, MD

"Being a BOSS MOM is about rising to the occasion so you can ensure your family always stays lifted up. It's not easy, but God instilled a special power inside all of us, that when diligently used matches His awesome power.

That's when the magic happens. BOSS MOM life is one of the most empowering blessings I have ever had the pleasure to encounter."

- Principle 3 -

Value of Unbalance

Principle 3

~

Embrace the Unbalance

It certainly looks like other moms have it all together, doesn't it? Perfectly prepared healthy and delicious snacks for their little ones, laundry washed, folded and put away, clean kitchens, made beds & beautifully arched brows!

How do they do it all? It may seem like everyone, but you have it together and that everyone has found their balance except for you. I know that's how I felt and this is normal.

In order for you to learn how to balance Motherhood, you get to first experience the opposite, *unbalance*. With time and practice, balance is a skill you'll learn and part of learning to balance is learning what like looks like when everything is unorganized and unbalanced.

Life is an absolute mess, filled with high emotions and sometimes chaos, this is normal. Through learning the unbalance of Motherhood, we are able to come up with ways to create balance in our lives, we understand how to spend our time and day to create more productive ways to handle everything that encompasses Motherhood.

Let's review some key points that help with embracing the unbalance of Motherhood.

This Time Will Pass

~

Your baby isn't sleeping through the night and you're surviving on cereal and coffee that you've microwaved three times in the last two hours. Yes, girl! I remember mornings where I had re-microwaved my coffee at least three times before I gave up on it and accepted the fact that I wasn't ever going to have a chance to have a seat and enjoy it.

That doesn't feel like balance, does it? But a couple of months of stale cereal or lukewarm coffee isn't the end of the world! Just because you're perhaps not drinking green smoothies or eating homemade granola doesn't mean that you're failing.
This time will pass and one day, eventually, you'll come back to or establish new food and nutrition routines. It may feel crazy and unbalanced now, but that's exactly part of learning to balance it all.

I look up, years have passed, and we are gearing up to getting my eldest ready for her first day of kindergarten. I still remember those sleepless nights with her when she was 4 months old and she had gone through sleep regression. My partner and I was operating off of thirty minutes of sleep and we were ready to kill each other. This goes to show how quickly time flies by. One minute you're hoping for a couple of hours of uninterrupted sleep, to now buying her first backpack. Enjoy these moments because they go by fast!

Perfection is an Illusion

~

Embracing the aspect of unbalance is accepting that everything will be a mess… constantly. That kitchen on Instagram may look perfect now, but the reality is that there's a stack of unsorted mail pushed off to the side just out of view and there will be dirty dishes in that sink later. It's easy to feel inadequate when we see others' perfect posts on social media but most of time, they aren't real because perfection isn't real. Again, for the people in the back: perfection isn't real!

If you're the sort of person who must have your kitchen or living room clean before going to bed, accept that life will happen in the morning. Life is

messy so are your living spaces, too. So will your clothes, your hair, and cars!
It is all part of the balancing act. Perfection is impossible and we might as well embrace the imperfections because that's what makes life beautiful.

Society will expect you to be a perfect mother, but perfection is impossible. Unfortunately, that doesn't stop society from thinking that moms can do everything and do it perfectly with a smile on your face. Surround yourself with love and friendship and the people who know and care about you. They are rooting for you and know you're doing your very best. Let their love drown out the noise of people telling you that you're not doing enough.

Relationships Change

~

Apart of the unbalance is that when you have a baby, it's possible that some of your friends already have children and some of your friends don't. When you enter this new, wonderful season of life, some of your friendships may change. Maintaining relationships after becoming a mother can be a tough balancing act. Accepting that relationships may not be the same, was the hardest thing for me to accept. I was a complete social butterfly before

Motherhood, I was out painting the town red anytime I got a chance. The change in my social habits took a blow to my Ego and my personal value.

I realized that most of my relationships were all based on something that was not authentic, in fact it was all based on a very shallow foundation. When it came to accepting that I was embarking on a journey that they were not on, or perhaps felt that I wasn't as useful to be around, the communication dwindled and eventually became nonexistent.

I questioned my relationships; how could I have been so naïve to think that I had something more meaningful with people around me. The transition of accepting new groups of people whom share the same values and priorities as I do help me cope with the feelings of inadequacy or questioning of my personal value or self-worth. There comes a time in life, where people grow together or grow apart… this is one of them. You will discover this in your journey of Motherhood. Don't judge yourself, be open and welcome the relationships that await your new chapter in life.

Conclusion

~

In order for you to learn order and routine, you must initially learn a life of chaos and the unbalance of Motherhood and of life. The one aspect you can count on in life is change, especially during Motherhood. Change in your lifestyle, the groups of people you once called your friends, daily routine, your diet, your household dynamic will change.

In order for you to develop systems that help you streamline your day to day or moments; you must adapt to the chaos of this journey. We must realize a life without those systems and how chaotic life can be. Only then, will we be able to cultivate better ways to operate within our busy mom lives.

Life & Motherhood is all about contracting and retracting, chaos and order, balance and unbalance.

NOTES:

~ The Boss Mom Community ~

Julie Ciardi

"I so often see mamas hand over their identity when they assume the name of mommy. I did this myself. We lose ourselves, our self-care, hobbies, passions because we put our children first always.

I have since learned that being More than Mommy is actually better for our kids. It shows our daughter's examples of the freedom to be themselves when they become a mom.

It shows our sons that their wives can do it all. It is my one wish that mamas give themselves more grace and attention without the guilt. You got this, mamas!"

- Principle 4 -

Realistic Sense of Reality

Principle 4

~

Realistic Sense of Reality

"Possess a realistic sense of how you show up in your life."

-M.H.

The Boss Mom Mentality is about having a realistic sense of her reality. There is danger in not knowing the truth of your reality and how you show up within it. It seems that an epidemic is upon us, that people think very highly of themselves, with nothing to show for it. Studies show that it is due to the lack of parenting and discipline received as a child with the combination of progress of the internet, social media and the decrease of real social interactions that people have with one another. We tend to warrant how well we are doing, by the *likes* we receive, or the *comments* and *shares* that get on a post. Not understanding that there is a level of narcissism that is sparked within a person, due to the falsehood of positive feedback.

Not allowing for an authentic foundation of your character, that encompasses your weakness, strengths, triumphs and challenges in your life to classify your identity, skews how you truly show up in your life. There is danger in this delusional sense of reality, as this skewed perception will trickle into your parenthood and how you raise your children and in result, how they see themselves and their reality. It is a vicious cycle, that keeps going on, generation to generation, unless *You*, take a stand for yourself and the future of your family.

Society is excellent at depicting Motherhood in a nice but largely false way. Most of the images that is depicted in the media of Motherhood is completely a fake resemblance of what a Boss Mom entails. The number of movies in theaters depicting moms who are dressed with their hair done serving their children five types of breakfast foods at the table before school is nice, but it's not the reality for most of us. Nor do we have the Kardashian lifestyle where we have assistance and nannies at our beckon call. In fact, most of us live a regular life where we work a day job.

We pay a daycare to watch our children and we are busy trying to get everything prepared for that night and the following day, while our children are begging for our attention, and this being a nightly ritual. Remove your delusion by having a realistic sense of your reality.

The problem is that some of us believe we are entitled to this lifestyle, or worst front like that is the kind of lifestyle we have when it's not reality at all. Having a false sense of reality can cause you to make decisions and draw conclusions that are from a place of an unrealistic sense of where you stand within your life. Get a grip on reality and operate from your you truly are in life. Only there will you find truth.

Let's look at some of those false depictions that society has portrayed on television and social media.

Your Body Bounces Right Back

~

Possibly the toughest reality is that our bodies change a lot during pregnancy and childbirth. It isn't bad, it's amazing. You grew a whole life in your womb and then brought it into the world. You truly earned those stretch marks and scars! Remember Kate Middleton's photo taken hours after she gave birth? She looked flawless even though her body has just undergone incredible trauma.

But you know what? Kate Middleton is English royalty and has hair, makeup, and wardrobe specialists on hand to make sure she looked as stunning as she did. That isn't the reality for most of us.

So many films and photos fail to show that your stomach takes time to go back to normal after pregnancy. Magazines edit out scars or airbrush stretch marks. But the reality is that birth is a huge event for a woman's body, and it will show. Don't' let society tell you that you aren't beautiful if you have scars, stretch marks or if you put on some weight. You've earned them and they tell a beautiful story.

The Boss Mom Mentality is about embracing who you are becoming in different parts of your life and that may mean accepting that your body is no longer the same and that's ok because the person you are is what makes you a Boss. No matter the car you drive, the job you have, or the stretch marks you possess, it doesn't make you any less of a person. Standing in your personal power is what a Boss Mom is and everything else is a nonfactor, including those stretch marks that you've gained through your pregnancies.

Motherhood is a Walk in The Park

~

Every media and entertainment outlets make Motherhood look like a breeze. Everyone looks well-rested, no one argues, and meals are perfectly prepared and nutritious. You will, of course, find that none of this is true. It's equally frustrating that a lot of the influencer parents, moms and dads, feed into this false depiction by only displaying the perfect images of their day to day lives.

It's completely false, as we all know that it takes a lot of energy to take care of little ones, let alone provide for your own mental, emotional and physical needs. Society has made us think that anything is easy if we just love enough or love hard enough.

No matter how much we love our children or our spouses or our families, challenges still exist. It's how you handle them that can encourage a mental growth, maturity and humility.

Hopefully, you already know it and won't learn the hard way. But, if you don't, society has fed you false expectations and that the daily struggle is beautiful and even the people making it look easy are working hard to make it look that way.

You Can Do It All

~

Between Mommy and Me swim classes, enrichment classes, doctors' visits, family time, and general life things like cleaning the house and preparing meals, there truly aren't enough hours in the day. There's a lot of pressure from society to do everything you can for your baby, and you should try your best to, but within reason. You and your little one will be too exhausted and crabby to enjoy your time together if you're filling every moment with activities.

It's a myth that all moms everywhere are doing it all. It's okay to relax for an hour before you start dinner or to walk through the local park instead of going to an expensive Mommy and Me class. You can enrich your baby's life without packing the days. Enjoy this time and take it slow. Your baby (and your mind and body) will thank you.

Moms Know Best

~

One of the biggest issues with a sense of delusion, is that people whom are so tied to their ego, being right or the best… is that they aren't open for improvement. Well let's change that, this is not The Boss Mom Mentality. Be open to constructive criticism, so you that you can learn to become a better version of yourself.

Develop a sense of humility, where you are open to other people's opinions, logically ration whether the information you receive makes sense and determine the best approach from there. Don't be completely closed off, but don't be completely naive, where you are taking everything at face value.

There is a level of screening you must put information through before accepting it. Be open to opinions, but don't let it be the end all or be all for you. Do some research, see if it is valid and make a decision if you want to implement it within your methods of parenting or raising your children if it makes sense to do so.

Conclusion

~

Don't believe the crap placed on IG stories and FB timelines of their perfectly dolled up photos. Society is full of false images of Motherhood. The reality is that it's a beautiful mess and that's worlds better than the carefully curated images on Pinterest and Instagram. Relinquish yourself of any false thought processes of what Motherhood is supposed to look like.

Be open that you could be wrong in somethings, wrong in your methods and that you can learn from someone more *knowledged* than you. Remove your ego, become friends with humility and know that there is always room for improvement.

Once you embrace the imperfections of Motherhood and within yourself, you can fully accept the rewarding journey. Don't contribute to the lie's society tells women about Motherhood.

Be real.

Be honest.

By doing so, you'll release yourself from society's lies and help other women, mothers, and your children live and portray authentic lives.

NOTES:

~ The Boss Mom Community ~

Sherry Ballan

"To all you mamas who worked those hard days and stressful hours, carrying your babies know that you've earned those stripes so wear them proudly. My tummy will probably never be as flat as it used to, and no lotion will mask these scars. But my stretch marks will be a beautiful reminder of how strong women are to handle pain and suffering even when they have no fight to give.

We all have different struggles and will never be completely prepared to face all tasks of Motherhood but at the end of each day we always prove to defeat the impossible and ready to do it even better the next! It wasn't till I became a mother of my own that I realized what my strongest capabilities were physically, mentally and emotionally. I have come to believe you are never given something you weren't meant to handle, and we are meant to be for them. So keep being the superstar they need."

- Principle 5 -

The Gift

Principle 5

~

The Gift

"Develop an appreciation for your chapter in Motherhood."

-M.H.

Our species has been bringing life into the world for thousands of years, but why is it still so scary to embark in this journey? Perhaps, because of the huge undertaking. You will be responsible for another person's life, responsible for how they grow up, responsible for teaching them the way of life and it is extremely terrifying.

What I needed to remind myself was, by being aware of the blessings that come with Motherhood, I can see the how to positively embrace this new chapter. Motherhood is one of the most emotionally challenging, physically draining and mentally exhausting chapters in any women's life and with attention and care, it could be the most magical time for you and your child.

Shining some positive light in this unknown journey, and can create some enthusiasm and faith that all will work out for you.

The Boss Mom Mentality embodies an understanding of the gifts that Motherhood offers.

Let's review some of the reason why Motherhood is an absolute gift!

Personal Growth

~

I go into detail about personal growth in Section 2, however I touch on it here because it is a huge part in becoming a Boss Mom.

Motherhood can encourage for some personal growth through the very emotional, physical and mental changes that each and every mom goes through. Motherhood is a powerful journey that begins from the moment we know we're carrying life once that pregnancy test reads positive.

These moments where our needs are met last, where we are taking care of another and where sometimes we may feel weak and alone, is where you can find the best moments to personally grow, experience your strongest parts of yourself and expand your capabilities and awareness.

My biggest challenge and blessing in disguise was that during my first months of Motherhood, I felt a sense of deep love for my baby while simultaneously feeling a strong sense of loneliness.

I didn't know what to make of it, aside from wondering how can I grow from this, what lesson is being shown to me during these lonely moments and ultimately, why does it bother me so much?

My curiosity for this grew as my loneliness grew, eventually understanding that connection was what I was seeking. Ultimately connection with myself.

Ah ha moment, as Oprah calls it.

Now I know what I need to work on! Moments like this opens the door to the keys of healing, the keys of revealing to yourself what YOU ultimately need to do to become *whole.*

I turned to writing all of this out in this book, it has been a rewarding feeling. Plenty of personal discoveries and a sense of self confidence has taken place because I've opened myself up throughout these challenging moments. Healing truly comes from within.

You must be open to seeing that these hardest moments in the journey of Motherhood, are exactly the moments that you need for growth and to become a better version of yourself.

According to Dr. Tsabary, Author of The Conscious Parent, *"When you experience everything as a potential teacher, you embrace anything life sends your way. You cease either being at war with life when it presents you with a challenge or being in love with it when it treats you kindly. Rather, you see both the dark and the light as opportunities for becoming a more conscious human being."*

Motherhood is a rewarding but a tough road. You can harness learning and energy that comes with being a mom to better yourself and become the people you want to model for your children.

Your child's development begins at home and stays with them, through their lives. Your child will be as good as you are, so constantly grow and develop to be the best version of yourself.

Unconditional Love

~

From the moment you see an image of a peanut shaped image possessing a heartbeat on the ultrasound screen, you start the journey to knowing your little one is growing and that you and only you are responsible for growing your child.

I felt that the unseen form of *being* within me created an emotional connection with my little one. Knowing that every breath I took, every piece of food that I consumed and even down to the emotions that I felt would have an effect on my unborn child.

The physical connection creates an undeniable attachment to something we haven't even met yet. There is a psychological affect that happens and pulls at our heartstrings. Your feeling deepens when you actually hear your child cry for the first time and you can see them, hug them and kiss them.

At that moment, anything they do is acceptable because there is a level of unconditional love that you feel … until they piss you off with their own opinions that go against your wishes, haha.

That's why you get them when they're adorable, innocent babies and by the time they're teenagers you'll love them too much to get too angry… at least, I think.

Having children ignites this level of unconditional love that, even if it lasts only for that moment or throughout the duration of your Motherhood, you'd experienced that kind of love for another…it's pretty magical.

True Colors

~

A blessing in disguise is when people fall off and new opportunities for more rewarding relationships presents themselves, that's a true gift When you have a child or start a family, there are times where you can't participate in the same activities as you once did. One of the changes in my journey of Motherhood was accepting that people will excuse themselves from my life, as I did not provide the same form of relationship that I once had.

It can be painful, as some old friends fade from your life but it ushers in a new, beautiful era of deepening relationships with other groups of people as your family expands.

Motherhood will challenge you in new, difficult ways and it's important to know who you can truly depend on. Luckily, those who don't support you will likely remove themselves from your life on their own and those who love and support you will be on the front lines when life gets tough.

This journey has a way of bringing out the true colors of those around us and ourselves. It isn't always easy, but it's always for the best.

What an amazing way to get people whom truly care about you and your child than making space by removing those whom didn't truly benefit you in your new chapter of Motherhood.

Like the popular song says, "Thank you, next!"

Conclusion

~

It is terrifying that you will be responsible for something so tiny and magnificent. A life… the purest form of life's creation that carries your blood and your DNA. A tiny, miniature you! Motherhood is hard and it's scary but it's also the greatest journey a woman can embark upon.

The true blessing is that your child has the whole world to grow into, learn from and create a magnificent life within. You get to provide the best life for them, the kinds of values and lessons that you've learned along the way from experience or perhaps give them what you didn't get to have as a child.

As a parent, you have the power to teach your child valuable life lessons, that can set them apart from others and can help create a successful life ahead. You can make the world a better place by teaching your children how to love, thrive and maximize their full potential and create a meaningful life for themselves.

I honor you for taking this step in becoming a better version of yourself during this exciting journey of Motherhood, now let's start Section Two!

NOTES:

~ The Boss Mom Community ~

Tsvetelina Hristov

"As a woman I feel there is a huge responsibility to be a great wife, mom, friend and so on. Since I could remember I was always a very competitive and independent person and never asked for help no matter what. I felt that asking for help made me weak.

Since I became a mom, help is needed more than ever. This is by far the hardest thing I had to do. Not only because you are a role model, but you feel you have to be able to achieve it all.

Slowly, I'm learning to ask for help. Even if this is not easy for my personality but I know is the right thing to do. Women are trying to fit into some "standards" as a mom and the reality is not what it seems. Everyone is doing things on their own pace. Understanding life in their own way.

One size doesn't fit us all. We are all different and the bottom line is working towards making our children (our future) respectful, well behaved, thankful and kind.

We are caught up so much on the social media and the idea of a perfect mom (it doesn't exist) that we truly forget who we are, what we like and what makes us happy. Slowly I'm learning to not compare myself to anyone because at the end of the day we are different. Live your life the way that makes you happy. Nobody knows you better than you."

Become a Boss Mom

- Section 2 -

Digging Deep

- Value of Journaling
- Opportunity for Growth
- Value of Self Awareness
- Value of Emotional Resilience
- Value of Adaptability

Section Two

~

Personal Development & Digging Deep

"Your success or failure depends entirely upon the quality of your thoughts."

-Robert Collier, The Secret of The Ages.

Section Two in The Boss Mom Mentality covers the connection between Personal Development, Motherhood and uncovering the barometer of your emotional health. What are the quality of your thoughts? Are they filled with positive or negative thoughts?

The Principles and Core Values ahead will give you some insight on the health of your thoughts, learn about your level of Self-Awareness and actionable tips to improve your thoughts and emotional health that is supportive to your Motherhood journey.

In order for any woman to be successful at being a mom and raising her children, you must have an emotionally balanced inner world. This is done by harnessing the power you have by controlling your thoughts and developing your self-awareness. The daily challenges of Motherhood can take a toll on your emotional health, looking inward is the solution to healing and becoming whole.

Personal Development is the gateway to reaching an emotionally balanced and healthy inner world and ultimately evoking The Boss Mom Mentality. Looking within and working on the pain and unhealed wounds that lay within your hearts and minds is beneficial to your Motherhood journey.

Ahead is the inner work that encourages for personal growth, emotional healing for a balanced Motherhood journey so that you can evoke an emotionally balanced and peaceful inner world.

- Principle 6 -

Value of Journaling

Principle 6

~

Value of Journaling

"I can shake off everything as I write, my sorrows disappear, my courage is reborn."

-Ann Frank

Journaling has played a huge role in my life, it has become my method of reflecting, a way for me to set goals, stay focused, emotionally decompress and stay attuned with what's going on in my current situations. The Boss Mom Mentality values reflection. I talk about reflecting and journaling a lot! Especially within the chapters ahead for reason.

During Motherhood, emotions are high sometimes and can seem like we have officially *lost it.* One minute we are happy, the next we are in tears and I have discovered the solution to taming our wild emotions… and that is through learning a new mindset and changing your thought process and calm your mind by the act of Journaling.

Why is Journaling Important to Motherhood?

Uncover the depths of your inner world through journaling about the circumstances of your life, change your mindset, your perceptions about Motherhood and emotional baggage that seems to keep coming up for you during this journey.

These rollercoaster feelings are normal, but in order for you to maintain a level of control and understanding of your emotional highs and lows, journaling is a successful method to accomplish this. Journal to improve your emotional health, resilience and become a mentally strong parent.

Initially, the concept of rewiring your brain sounds scientific and somewhat impossible unless guided by a professional, but there is scientific proof that its really simple and it is achieved by journaling.

It takes consistent action outside of your habits that make simple changes difficult to accomplish.

Write in a Journal

~

As you read the following Principles, I recommend to journal about what comes up for you and as we will cover some meaningful topics.

The act of journaling can actually rewire your inner beliefs, your behaviors thought processes, improve your self-confidence, building new neural pathways for better understanding, evoking a creative approach to problem solving, causing for better results and a happier you.

Below is an illustration of the Brain and reviewing terms that will be referenced of how the brain gets rewired through journaling.

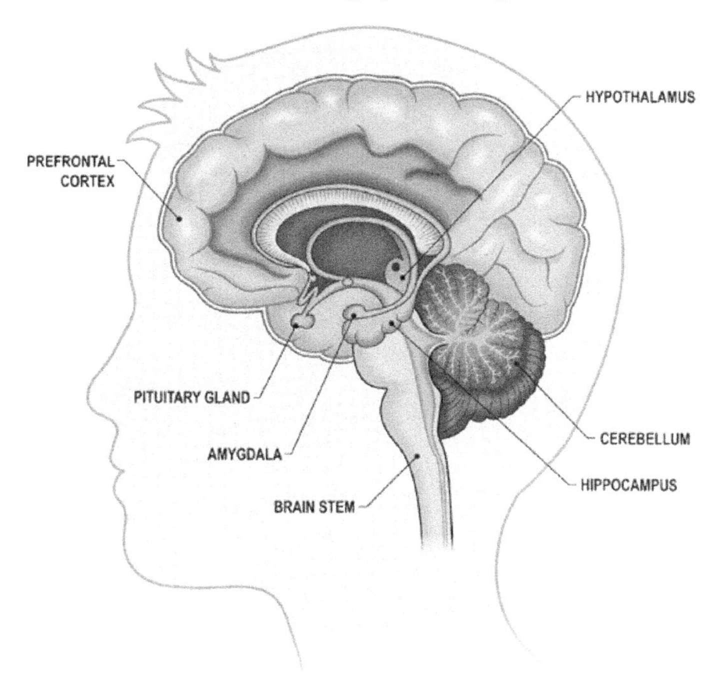

Amygdala

~

The Amygdala sits in the middle of your brain, a peanut size tissue that is largely responsible for processing of emotions, fear, survival instincts and memory.

When this part of the Brain is triggered, the fight or flight response within your Brain is activated. This part of the Brain controls our primitive and archaic tendencies which tells us to go into survival mode if we need to protect ourselves.

Prefrontal Cortex

~

The Prefrontal Cortex sits right above your eye sockets. This is a part of the brain where thinking and cognition takes place where we want to train our brain to draw conclusions from.

The prefrontal cortex is the most recent, newly developed part of the Brain that our species has created for cognition, rationalizing, social behavior and personality traits.

It takes some time for outside information to pass through the different parts of the brain before getting to the prefrontal cortex where ration takes place. Journaling or the process of meditating can help with building and strengthening this process.

Brain Stem

~

The Brain Stem is the initial part of the brain where information travels to. This is the part of the Brain that communicates with the body. The Brain Stem sends signals to the body based on the information it is receiving.

This part of the brain controls the basic body functions like breathing, swallowing, heart rate, blood pressure, consciousness, and either sleep or awake. All species possess a Brain Stem, which is another archaic part of the Brain that response with impulse.

Updating our Supercomputers

~

"Since most people cannot see the brain, it is often left out of the equation of our personal lives. Yet, it is the core of our personal universe."
-Daniel G. Amen M.D., *The Brain in Love*

There is a very interesting connection between computers and the Brain.

According to Jim Kwik, CEO & Founder of Kwik Learning, the Brain is essentially a supercomputer processing at the capacity of what we've intentionally and unintentionally taught it to operate from.

Just like your computers you work off of, if you don't update your programs from time to time, we are working off of an older version of the system. As I mentioned previously, we must become adaptable and be willing to change to perform at your highest potential.

Journaling is one of the ways to intentionally teach and rewire new processes in any given chapter of your life. You can intentionally, pick and choose what you want your brain to operate off of.

The Brain and the concept of rewiring your thoughts, causing different emotions, creating a new behavior that can lead to intentional results is possible. The possibility of changing our results in our lives by understanding the power of our Brains is extremely possible and easier than you would assume.

Primitive Beings

~

"Although human beings today live in a technology-driven world of galactic voyages and virtual realities, we still face everyday life with deeply embedded traits of Stone Age hunter-gatherers."

-Robert K. Cooper, The Other 90%

It's been a long journey to get to the evolution of our species, but that doesn't mean our brains have caught up to our modern-day problems and skills to solving them.

The channels of where information is *first* received in the brain is through the archaic and more primitive part of the brain called the Brain Stem. It takes a longer timeframe for information to get to the Prefrontal Cortex of where thinking and cognition take place.

By nature, we respond to problems, issues and any concern in an archaic fashion and not thought out, due to brain stem. The problem with this is that if we don't train ourselves to sit with information, let it marinate in your mind before responding, the less your results will be beneficial.

The act of journaling allows you this power. It creates an awareness of the delay in action and to hold off on your instinctive responses and to really *think* about the way you respond to any situation.

In short, the archaic part of your brain is trained to react instantly, in survival mode or fight or flight tendency. Journaling can help us slow down the archaic part of our brains and increase it's supercomputer capacity so we can react in better, more thoughtful and healthier ways to the situations around us.

According to Dr. Tsabary, she writes in her book The Conscious Parent; *"By silently witnessing our thoughts and feelings, we learn to accept them as they are, allowing them to rise and fall within us without resisting them or reacting to them."*

So that you can allow these archaic responses to subside will better aid you with rationalizing each situation and responding in a beneficial and more logically way.

Information Discarders

~

The brain uses 30% of the human body's energy for it to process, receive data, analyze it and draw conclusions. One of the ways the brain conserves energy is that it automatizes anything and everything and disregards things that the brain thinks is unimportant or not useful. It will literally not include information to you, if it thinks it is unimportant.

For example, I've been driving for almost two decades now, with all the experience I have had, my brain is now able to automatize the act of driving, I don't have to think hard to drive my car. It has become automatic. Have you ever thought about the areas in your life that has become automatic?

Automatizing our day to day is good for us but may not be beneficial for our relationships and that is where Journaling falls into place.

The act of Journaling can actually create awareness of these patterns or automatized responses so that we can truly respond from our hearts, values and what's important to us for more meaningful relationships with others and ourselves. It forces us to slow down and think about the things our brains may have put on autopilot.

Millions of Thoughts

~

Since our brains are supercomputers, it can be a lot of thoughts spinning around in any given person's mind at any given time. According to a documentary: *Secrets of The Human Brain*, the average person speaks to themselves at a rate of 300 to 1000 words per minute and a lot of the time, these inner conversations are driven by the part of the brain that operates fear called the Amygdala.

Journaling about our goals and future enlists the rational part of our brain, the Frontal Lobe, to assist with achieving such goal.

The goal is to learn that our quick responses don't benefit us. It is the response that is based off of love and reason that does. It takes patience, consistent efforts and making this a habit of how to respond within each moment.

The process redirects the energy from the Amygdala creating a more focused, calm and harmonious mental state.

"When intention is repeated, that creates habit. The more an intention is repeated, the more likely it is that the universal consciousness will create the same pattern and manifest intention the physical world."

-Deepak Chopra, Spontaneous Fulfillment of Desire.

Conclusion

~

Our brains are wild and can drive us to live very unhappy lives if left unguided. Even though we have evolved into such a domestic society, our brains still operate archaically, responding in survival mode.

We must actively work on our minds, be mindful of the processor it's running off of, be cognizant of our responses to people and situations by journaling.

Journaling is a great tool to tame the "*monkey mind*", as Dalai Lama calls it. Get on the right track and cultivate a life with meaningful relationships with others and most importantly, with yourself. After all, it's not what happens to us that defines us, but it's how we *deal* with it, that does.

NOTES:

"The greatest discovery of my generation is the fact that human beings can alter their lives by altering their attitudes of mind."

-William James

- Principle 7 -

Opportunity for Growth

Principle 7

~

Opportunity for Growth

~

"The growth of wisdom may be gauged accurately by the decline of ill-temper."

-Friedrich Nietzche

It is no joke, that Motherhood forces you to deal with your unhealed wounds and brings up emotional challenges. My emotional baggage came up for me, time and time again when the people closest to me would let me down or if I had a trying day with my child or an argument with my partner. My world was quickly turned upside down and it took me some time to get back to normal.

I needed to figure out a way to take these moments and actually learn from them. Instead of it happening to me, I took charge of the moments by reflecting and seeing how I could improve in each moment, through self analysis and Personal Development.

Why is Personal Development Important in Motherhood?

Moments in Motherhood ushers in opportunities to become whole even in ways that we don't want to uncover.

This is an incredible journey and if you do the work, can change you in ways you never imagined. It's tough, it's challenging, but it's an incredible avenue for Personal Development if you're open to it. Moments where you feel disappointment or strong negative feelings are great opportunities to look within to see what areas you need growth in.

According to Dr. Tsabary, she writes in her book The Conscious Parent; *"The process of losing our reactivity accelerates as our awareness deepened."*

Your children's greatest lessons will be taught at home. It is important to be mindful about what they're learning from us. Therefore, using our time to develop ourselves as people and as mothers will benefit us, our families, and society.

Opportunity for Growth

~

"That which does not kill us, makes us stronger."

-Fredrick Nietzche

That saying above by the great Nietzche, has a level of truth to it. However, the entire truth is, what doesn't kill you, forces you to adapt, and you create ways to handle the situation. We grow and become accustomed to that specific stress or problem.

We are always growing and adapting, and there is no difference in Motherhood. We grow, we adapt, and we become stronger. The question is, at what level are you going to reach?

A level of mediocrity or a level of a Boss Mom?

You can easily give your child the bare necessities, but to be a Boss, you're giving invaluable life lessons, role modeling a strong woman and exercising one's own moral compass and self-worth. To get there, we are taking the Personal Development route. Digging deep to honestly work on your weaknesses and exemplifying your strengths.

Let's look at the main points of Personal Development to encourage The Boss Mom Mentality and growth.

Self-Awareness

~

If Motherhood teaches us anything, it's seeing that your lack of self-awareness will reflect your emotional stability or instability. This is one of the most important parts of the book.

That if you don't get anything, this is the one thing that I want you to get. *The depth of your self-awareness is in correlation with how well you handle Motherhood and its challenges.*

We will review this ahead as it is a powerful way to shift your approach to situations in your journey.

Emotional Resilience

~

Your ability to bounce back after emotional setbacks is key to when you are at high stresses during your mom life.

Covering this topic is important tool when you discover the connection, your personal power and how to effectively *mom* during the days, weeks and months ahead.

Conclusion

~

When we focus on improving ourselves through Personal Development, we literally can change our relationships with the people around us but also with ourselves, not only do we prosper, but so do our children and families.

The one thing to get about personal growth and self-development is that it is not a massive task or change, but it's the little actions, the little shifts in your behaviors that create positive results when done consistently.

As parents to your children, you have the power to positively or negatively influence your child. Use that power and work on Personal Development to improve yourself, your inner dialogue and belief of yourself so that it is a positive influence.

NOTES:

~ The Boss Mom Community ~

Yvette Garcia

"The only limits we have are the ones we give ourselves. Our children need you to follow your dreams so we, as mothers can pour back into them and show them that anything is possible.

Our children will imitate you for the good or bad, so let them see you try, let them see you fail forward until you find success. That is true impact."

- Principle 8 -

Value of Self Awareness

Principle 8

~

Value of Self-Awareness

"Until you make the unconscious conscious, it will direct your life and you will call it fate."

-Dr. Carl Jung

One of the challenges in my life, is not knowing my strengths and who I truly am, my darkness and all that make up my identity. To bridge this gap, I read up on the psychology of the mind, how your emotional wellbeing is connected to unhealed wounds of the past. For true growth, looking inward is key.

"The emotional self thrives on ignorance", as Robert Greene states in the Laws of Human Nature.

To get a hold of our tendencies of being over-emotional and highly explosive in our lives, we must bridge the gap of ignorance by cultivating a strong sense of self-awareness.

A woman's ability to possess The Boss Mom Mentality is based off of the level and depth of her self-awareness. The better you know yourself, the better you can problem solve, and handle situations life throws at you. Becoming self-aware and knowing who you are, is imperative if your goal is teaching your children to become emotionally balanced, confident, and self-aware individuals.

What is Self-Awareness and why is it important in Motherhood?

Self-awareness relates to self-control. The more self-aware we are, the more we are able to self-regulate our emotions in times of high stress like in Motherhood. How would anyone teach another how to be something, if they themselves don't have any idea on how to practice this within their own lives.

The inner work begins with us. We are not here to provide our children with the bare minimum; shelter, food, and clothes on their backs. We have a larger responsibility to teach our offspring about discovering their values, their strengths, know their weakness and to master the skill of self-regulation.

Define

Self-Awareness (n)

Conscious knowledge of one's own character, feelings, motives and desires.

Internal & External Self-Awareness

~

Becoming truly self-aware is possessing a delicate balance of ***internal self-awareness***; which is defined as a representation of how clearly, we see our own values, passions, aspirations and how it fits with our environment, reactions and how it impacts others. ***External self-awareness*** which is an understanding how other people view us, in terms of those same factors listed above.

Most think that if you are high on external self-awareness, you would automatically be high on the internal self-awareness.

However, studies show that people rank high on one and low on the other. It is detrimental to have an imbalance of external and internal self-awareness, as this causes a level of *narcissism* or the opposite, a person of low *self-esteem.* Unfortunately, this imbalance is more common in our society.

Thus, the balance between the two create a healthy level of one's Self Awareness.

Core Values

"When our individual values don't fit with the life we're leading or the direction we're moving, we withhold our best and feel empty or stressed."

-Robert K. Cooper, The Other 90%

~

Core Values is defined as the fundamental beliefs of a person or organization. These guiding Principles dictate behavior and can help people understand the difference between *right* and *wrong.*

Determining your Core Values means to get to know what is *important* to you, what are your emotional boundaries and why your relationships play out in your life the way that they do.

If you don't know what your Core Values are, it's best that you do some self-discovery in this area. How can you show up for your children, teach them about healthy relationships, if you aren't able to identity and command that for yourself? Our Core Values determine the decisions you make, the relationship you tolerate and most importantly how you love yourself. Thus, this concept is the corner stone of self-awareness.

Core Values can include being patient, responsibility, respect, justice, fairness, family, connection, integrity, honesty, and trust.

How to determine what your Core Values are is simple. Discover what you find important by taking notice of the emotions that come up for you in different scenarios. Observe your emotions during high stresses or feelings of unworthiness. For instance, as a working mom and a side author, I noticed that I wasn't spending as much time with my kids as I would like. Days and weeks would go by, where I felt that I didn't spend time with my children, left me feeling worthless and a strong sense of guilt.

These negative feelings are clues to Core Values that aren't being met. In this case, the Core Value was *Quality Time with Family*. To bridge the gap, I committed a portion of my time after work with my kids and take them somewhere special on weekends. I also ensure that when I am with my children, that I am as *present* as possible.

What instance have you had where your emotions would signal to you that a Core Value is not being met?

Negative or Positive emotions signifies a Core Value that you find important. Pay attention to them and don't ignore them. This is the window to be able to create a meaningful life for yourself and your family.

According to Susan David, author of Emotional Agility, *emotions are guidepost to what we find important in your life and your relationships*. If your emotions signal you in a negative way, it's usually a sign that something needs to change or be addressed.

Think about some of your Core Values. What are Core Values that define who you are and what you stand for?

Core Values

1.________________________

2.________________________

3.________________________

4.________________________

~~

Determining this about yourself will allow you to start implementing personal boundaries within your relationships. Cultivating a sense of self awareness and valuing who you are means you get to place importance on your Core Values and holding those around you accountable to respect those Core Values.

If your Core Values aren't met by the people, you're in relationships with, that means you are not holding your Core Values steadfast and standing your ground, thus reflecting poor self-confidence and a low sense of self-worth.

On the other hand, if you are quick to communicate your displeasure about disrespect of any kind, due to crossing of one of your Core Values, that tells people that you know who you are, what you will stand for and that you have personal boundaries set for how you want be treated. This level of self-awareness creates for thriving relationships in your life.

The scary thing is that people will continue living life and not giving any true notice to their emotions and allowing for people to undermine their worth or value. This causes an emotional turmoil in any person's self-worth or self-importance. By being aware of your emotional guide, you can stand up for yourself and have healthier relationship with yourself and with others, increasing your sense of self-worth.

People will either respect that or no longer be in a relationship with you. Either way, it's a win because you stand in your power thus giving you self-confidence and loving who you are. This expression of self-love will resonate within how you treat other people, how you treat your children and they see how they themselves should be treated.

Emotional Triggers

Knowing your darkness helps you understand the Darkness in others.

-Dr. Carl Jung

~

Emotional Triggers are connected to how you respond during moments where one of your emotional responses get stressed due to a particular challenging situation. You respond poorly if you are not aware of your Emotional Triggers and the opposite if you are well aware of them.

As a woman raising children, you must know what ticks you off, so in moments where you feel like you are reaching that point, you have the power to reel yourself back in and not lash out at your loved ones.

List some things that are Emotional Triggers for you.

Emotional Triggers

1.__________________________

2.__________________________

3.__________________________

4.__________________________

~~

Understanding your emotional triggers are a part of taking your power back and learning that you have the ability to respond in more beneficial ways. Rather than react in a negative way, take a step back, see if this is just an emotional trigger response.

The power lies within the moments before you respond when you are triggered. In Principle #7, is an illustration of the brain showing the different parts of the brain that reflect the primitive parts and the more rational parts of the brain.

The brain stem is the first place where information enters. The brain stem is the archaic part of the brain where, archaic and survival mode behavior originates from. If you let yourself respond instantly, that means you are allowing the primitive side to respond to the situations and circumstances of your life. I can guarantee that 9 out of 10 responses, will be reactionary and is based on defense or in a survival mode mindset.

However, if you allow the information to pass through the brain stem and the amygdala, to reach the prefrontal cortex, where your ability to rationalize takes place, then you are able to draw rationalized conclusions by thinking about the bigger picture and make decisions that are more productive and beneficial for you and the people whom are directly affected by your decisions.

"Trust your feelings! – But feelings are nothing but final or original; behind feelings there stand judgements and evaluations which we inherit in the form of ... inclinations, aversions ... The inspiration born of a feeling is the grandchild of a judgement – and often of a false judgement! – and in any event not a child of your own! To trust one's feelings – means to give more obedience to one's grandfather and grandmother and their grandparents than to the gods which are in us: our reason and our experience."

-Friedrich Nietzsche

Benefits of Waiting Before Responding

~

Perspective comes overtime time and the solution is usually very simple, to draw those solutions forward can be a complex process. Only time and allowing yourself to think can help you approach complex situations in a more mindful way. Practice the ability to *wait, sit & think* about your responses and break the habit and need to immediately respond.

1| Productive Responses

You make better decisions during high stressed moments. Allowing for more beneficial results and outcomes.

Relationships around you become stronger because you can problem solve better. Allowing for productive communication with others and being open enough to share your concerns or any feelings that you may be experiencing.

Rationalizing information and becoming more aware of the bigger picture allows for you to come up with conclusions that benefit you and the people directly or indirectly affected by the situation.

2| Positive Role Model

The way you handle situations and problem solve in your life is how your child will handle problems and situations in their life.

Your child responds to situations the way they've seen the people in their lives respond to their challenging moments. They literally will copy this, at least until they can start thinking for themselves and making their own decisions.

Even until then, your child will observe how you were as a role model or lack thereof when they become adults themselves and look back at moments within their childhood. Your child sees how you respond in these moments and will mimic how you are being.

Different Approaches to Self-Awareness

~

There many ways that you can learn about yourself and the depths of your self-awareness. I've gathered data from Psychologist, researchers, therapist, thought leaders and studies performed on a wide range of people across a span of time, with various backgrounds, situations and circumstances to uncover useful information to understand self-awareness on a grander scale.

There are different ways to measure your self-awareness. First, we will review the scale of consciousness. Going over the different human emotion and reviewing their calibrated measurement according to Dr. Hawkins, based on his study in Power vs. Force and how it impacts our reality.

Second, we will review Four Self-Awareness Archetypes, revealing the differences between those whom deal with setback's in life better than those whom take more time to get through those similar hardships. There is a clear difference between those two groups of people, and we will review what those differences are and how to apply that in your life.

Three, we will review the Four Personality Disc styles that help with better communication and practice on being adaptable with how you communicate with whom you are in a personal or professional relationship with.

Your Energy

~

Do you notice people's energy from a mile away? Or if a person enters the room, conversations change because their energy is off? People can truly suck the energy from you and some people have the power to emit love and grace. We all emit a level of energy and we exude different types of energy in different categories of our lives.

We may feel love and joy for our children but feel guilt with our romantic relationships or we may exude fear or pride in the workplace. These types of energy are worth looking into on a deeper level and understanding why we emit these types of energy in different parts of our lives.

In the book, Power vs. Force by Dr. David Hawkins, M.D. Ph.D. a nationally renowned psychiatrist, physician, researcher, spiritual teacher, lecturer and bestselling author, goes into detail on how energy is calibrated and emits a measurable energy, that can't be ignored.

Dr. Hawkins reveals actual calibrated measurements for each human emotion… energy is what we all exude one way or another within the following scale of consciousness and different categories of our lives.

Dr. Hawkins's Scale of Consciousness

The scale is based on the calibrations measured by Dr. Hawkins research.

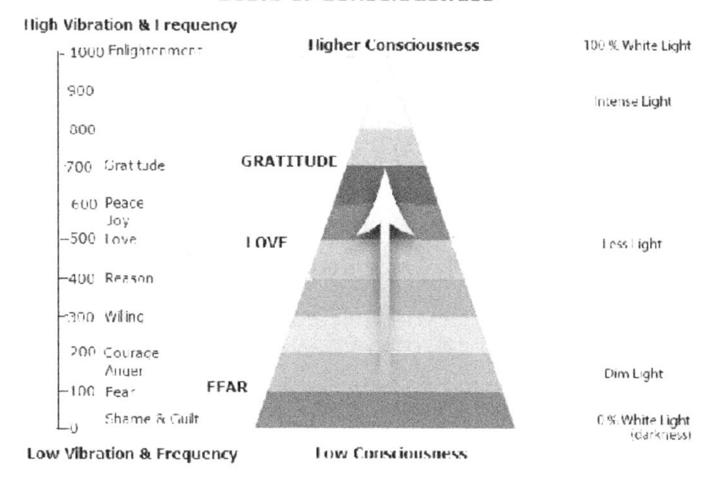

In the book, he states, "*It is important to remember that the calibration figures do not represent an arithmetic, but logarithmic, progression. Thus, the level 300 is not twice the amplitude of 150; it is 300 to the 10th power (10^{300}). Therefore, an increase of even a few points represents a major advance in power; the rate of increase in power as we move up the scale is therefore enormous.*"

Dr. Hawkins explains that there are levels to consciousness, and he shares the scale of consciousness from the lowest, *Shame* to the highest, *Enlightenment*.

It is beneficial to acquaint yourself with the concept of energy, where each energy lies within Dr. Hawkins Scale of Consciousness and its measurements. Reflect on how you operate in your lives with regards to the kind of energy you bring forth.

Dr. Hawkins's Scale of Consciousness Explained

~

Energy Level 20: Shame

Defined as a painful emotion caused by consciousness of guilt, shortcoming or impropriety.

**Those who operate from deep shame, operate at the lowest frequency vibration and have the worst mindset, generally those who have suffered from sexual abuse or similar trauma will operate off of this energy level, unless treated through therapy. **

Energy Level 30: Guilt

Defined as making someone feel guilty, especially in order to induce them to do something, or fact of having committed a specified or implied crime or offense. Or can be defined as feelings that you've done a terrible thing and that energy is exuded as Guilt.

Energy Level 50: Apathy

Defined as lack of interest, enthusiasm or concern.

Energy Level 75: Grief

Defined as a deep sorrow, especially that caused by someone's death.

Energy Level 100: Fear

Defined as an unpleasant emotion caused by the belief that someone or something is dangerous, likely to cause pain, or a threat.

Energy Level 125: Desire

Defined as a strong feeling of wanting to have something or wishing for something to happen.

Energy Level 150: Anger

Defined as a strong feeling of annoyance, displeasure, or hostility.

Energy Level 175: Pride

Defined as to be especially proud of (a particular quality or skill).

Energy Level 200: Courage

Defined as the ability to do something that frightens one.

Interestingly, politicians operate an energy lower than 200 or max of 200

Energy Level 250: Neutrality

Defined as the state of not supporting or helping either side in a conflict, disagreement, etc.

Energy Level 300: Willingness

Defined as the quality or state of being prepared to do something; readiness.

Energy Level 350: Acceptance

Defined as the action of consenting to receive or undertake something offered.

Energy Level 400: Reason

Defined as think, understand, and form judgments by a process of logic.

Energy Level 500: Love

Defined as feeling deep affection for (someone).

Energy Level 540: Joy

Defined as a feeling of great pleasure and happiness.

Self Help groups or Personal Development Organizations as a unit, operate at this level

Energy Level 600: Peace

Defined as freedom from disturbance; tranquility.

Energy Level 700 to 1000: Enlightenment

Defined as the action of enlightening or the state of being enlightened.

Those considered Mahatma Gandhi, Mother Theresa's of the world, operate at this level.

~~~

It is important to realize how we show up, energetically in our lives… are you shameful in some areas? Are you prideful in other areas? Are you more loving and patient other areas?
~~~

In the different categories of life, Health, Relationships, Marriage or Romance, Career, Finance, Family, we all show up differently. Taking inventory of what energy, we carry in each category of our lives is a great way to deepen our level of self-awareness, be able to improve our weaknesses and show up for our children in the best ways possible.

Only here will you be able to make personal adjustments and ensure that you can show up with higher levels of energy to truly operate at a higher level and evoke the Boss Mom in you.

Rate Your Energy

~

Honestly reflect the kind of energy that you emit in the different categories below… no one will see this unless you decide to share it with others…. It would be a disservice if you approached this exercise with dishonest answers. Be honest and write down what your true number is.

How do you show up in the following areas

(provide a number between 1-10, 10 being the highest, 1 being the lowest.)

Parenting ____________________

Work _______________________

Marriage ____________________

Family ______________________

Health ______________________

Finances ____________________

~~

As stated earlier, knowing how you show up in each area of your life is a great way to start taking inventory of what's working and what's not. Then making improvements where you see fit, bridge the gaps that are lacking and emphasize what is working in your life.

The point of this is to increase your level of awareness when it comes the energy you emit and experience in each area of your life. How you show up in your life, is a reflection of the trajectory of your life and is an example to your children and how they should or should not show up in their own lives. They learn best from the person whom raises them… let's show them how to operate at a higher frequency, from love, joy and happiness.

Group A vs. Group B Research

~

Dr. Tasha Eurich had a profound take on self-awareness and the approach in which we try to understand self-awareness.

Dr. Eurich is an organizational psychologist, researcher and NY Times bestselling author. She researched how people differ in problem solving and how their ability to problem solving is a key to their level of self-awareness.

The question she researched was:

How quickly does people overcome life changing setbacks like death or loss of a loved one?

Eurich's research revealed that those whom were able to recover quicker from this kind of setback asked a different question from the group that struggled for a longer period of time due to thus set back.

What was that profound difference?

The difference was the *question* that they asked themselves.

Group A; which was the group that took longer to recover asked *Why*.

Group B; whom was able to recover quicker from the setback, asked *How*.

How we make the most of our personal setbacks instead of asking ***Why*** we had that personal setbacks are what set the two groups apart.

Those whom asked How, was more self-aware then those who asked Why.

Dr. Eurich, states that by asking Why, people would go down a path of, could have, would have & should have thinking and is defined as a negative and less beneficial approach. Perhaps, they could have done something different to lead to a different result. Asking Why represents living in the past, which perpetuates the Detrimental Loop (reference Principle #13).

While asking How represented a person creating anew. *"How do I make the most of this situation?"*

A pivotal *How* question allows the person to propel forward in their setback, instead of stewing in their problem, the approach is **solution oriented**.

The illustration of the 4 archetypes play off of each other's' qualities. Study the 4 quadrants and see where you fall under.

Four Self Awareness Archetypes

The Four Self-Awareness Archetypes

This 2x2 maps internal self-awareness (how well you know yourself) against external self-awareness (how well you understand how others see you).

	Low external self-awareness	High external self-awareness
High internal self-awareness	**INTROSPECTORS** They're clear on who they are but don't challenge their own views or search for blind spots by getting feedback from others. This can harm their relationships and limit their success.	**AWARE** They know who they are, what they want to accomplish, and seek out and value others' opinions. This is where leaders begin to fully realize the true benefits of self-awareness.
Low internal self-awareness	**SEEKERS** They don't yet know who they are, what they stand for, or how their teams see them. As a result, they might feel stuck or frustrated with their performance and relationships.	**PLEASERS** They can be so focused on appearing a certain way to others that they could be overlooking what matters to them. Over time, they tend to make choices that aren't in service of their own success and fulfillment.

SOURCE DR. TASHA EURICH

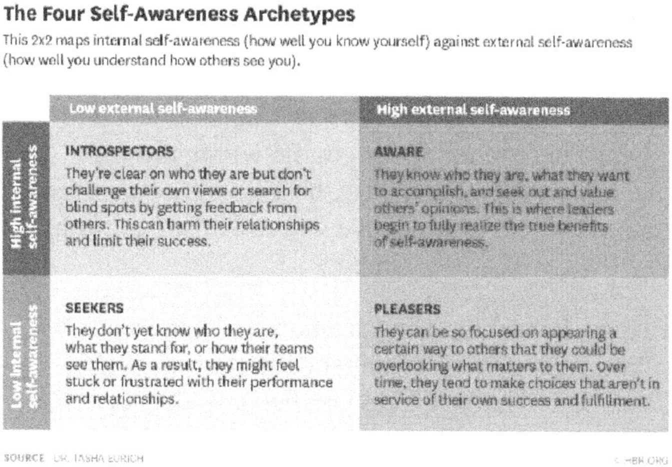

These 4 Archetypes review how different people problem solve.

Understanding where you lie within these Archetypes is key to how well you know yourself and how to effectively problem solve during challenging moments.

In order for you to get to know yourself well you must determine where you lie within these 4 quadrants. Ask your spouse, best friend, coworkers and boss where they believe you fall in and go from there.

Take an honest look and see how you can improve yourself and how to better communicate with others. This will help you become a better communicator with your child and those whom are important around you for a thriving and fulfilling relationship.

DISC Personality Style

~

Another way to get better understanding of your self-awareness level is knowing where you fall within the DISC Style and how you receive and give information, how you communicate and receive information in your relationships, both professionally and personally. The DISC Illustration shows the four quadrants that people fall under and their natural tendencies.

Dr. William Moulton Marston, a psychologist and author of *Emotions of Normal People*, formulated 4 different ways to categorize the most common characteristics of humanity. The DISC personality style was primarily used to uncover communication style in the workplace to create higher production and profitability. But sooner than later, it was realized that this study revolutionized the idea of understanding people and the psychology of human dynamics beyond the workplace.

Dr. Marston's *Emotions of Normal People* also included two dimensions that influenced people's emotional behavior. The first dimension is whether a person views his environment as favorable or unfavorable. The second dimension is whether a person perceives himself as having control or lack of control over his environment. Very similar to the concept stated in the earlier Principle, external and internal self-awareness.

Active
Dominant
Direct
Decisive
Doer
Domineering
Demanding
Inspirational
Interactive
Interesting
Impulsive
Irritating
Dominant
Influential
D
I
Task Focus
People Focus
C
S
Compliant
Steady
Compliant
Cautious
Careful
Conscientious
Calculating
Condescending
Steady
Stable
Supportive
Sincere
Slow
Sensitive
Reflective

D.I.S.C. Styles

Dominant, Influential, Steady & Compliant

~

Dr. Marston's way of analyzing human dynamics is titled DISC styles because, it is after each of the personality traits; Dominant, Influential, Steady and Compliant.

The better you know where you and others fall within the 4 quadrants, the better you are able to communicate your needs and effectively have working the relationships around you.

Good communication is all about being able to know who you are speaking with, how to *figuratively* meet them where they are so that they can trust you to listen to your needs and that you can effectively communicate and vice versa.

Being versatile and communicating with others based on their communication style allows for a thriving relationship, where both people are getting what they want because communication is clear and goals can be achieved.

The DISC styles help you with understanding the types of personalities people possess and how to work with each one. Let us take a deeper look at how each characteristic looks like in real life, their challenges and strengths and how to communicate with each type.

~ Dominant (D) ~

Whom are D's & their Strengths?

Dominant people are drivers, results oriented, they like things done NOW. They can come off arrogant, a bully at times, expecting results sooner than later and can be intimidating.

Strong (D)'s are usually leaders of the household; in their social groups and organizations they work for. They hold high positions because of their fearlessness to drive results.

Challenges of D's

They are intimidating, they can come off as bully's they are pushy and don't really think twice about other people's feelings. They are more concerned with results.

How to Communicate with D's:

Straightforwardness is what they appreciate. No BS, they can see right through this, be honest and direct with what you want from them.

Instrumental Characteristics:

Direct

Decisive

Driver

Doer

Detrimental Characteristics:

Domineering

Demanding

Intimidating

Bully

~ Influential (I) ~

Whom are I's & their Strengths?

Influential's are usually the highly enthused, highly emotional people. They promote and market everything and anything that they are currently into. They are *feelings* based and run their decisions based on emotions.

Strong (I)'s are people found as the talkers of the group or the social butterflies, they like being in the limelight and love praise and attention. They are great with clients and build rapport well.

Challenges of (I)'s

They may make decisions based on their emotions, which aren't always long term beneficial nor reliable. They ride the rollercoaster of emotions and you may have to deal with their extreme UPS and extreme DOWNS, which can be exhausting.

How to Communicate with I's:

Be exciting, be theatrical when asking for what you want.

Instrumental Characteristics:

Inspirational

Interactive

Interesting

Expressive

Detrimental Characteristics:

Impulsive

Irritating

Irate

Irrational

Flighty

Emotional

~ Steady (S) ~

Whom are S's & their Strengths?

Steady's are usually the supporters in their groups, they are constantly checking in on people to see if they are comfortable. They are givers and care takers; they take everyone's feelings into consideration. Making others happy is important to them, they run from conflict and can't stand bad energy. Strong (S)'s are generally busy making people and comfortable.

Challenges of S's:

They are more concerned with making others happy and can compromise their own happiness to achieve this. People of strong S's may put aside their goals, needs and wants to achieve the happiness for others. Overtime, this will create resentment within their relationships.

How to Communicate with S's:

Since the S's are busy making people happy, all you need to do is communicate what you need help with. If they find your relationship worth the effort, they will gladly do the favor you are asking for.

Instrumental Characteristics:

Stable

Supportive

Sincere

Amiable

Detrimental Characteristics:

Slow

Sensitive

~ Compliant (C) ~

Whom are C's & their Strengths?

Compliant's are the analytical of the group, they are mathematicians and engineers. They love facts figures; they enjoy analyzing data and information.

They do not enjoy making decisions. They would rather think of all possible scenarios, then come up with conclusions. Strong (C)'s are driven by data.

Challenges of C's:

They have trouble making decisions, they are always on the fence and will need to brainstorm or bounce ideas to themselves or a trusted person multiple times before making a decision.

Once the decision is made, they will question if they've made the most beneficial decision. I know… this is annoying, my partner is a strong C.

How to Communicate with C:'s

Fill your request with data, information, facts and figures. In order for them to help with anything you must give them information to analyze.

Be patient because it may take some time before a response or a final decision is made. You may also get several options to analyze from the Complaint, as this is his way of avoiding making a decision and in the end, leaving it up to you to make the decision.

Instrumental Characteristics:

Cautious

Careful

Conscientious

Analytical

Detrimental Characteristics:

Calculating

Condescending

Hard to Make Decision

Conclusion

~

Understanding the power of Self-Awareness is the key to unlocking your truest and highest potential in how you show up for your kids, how you show up in your life and the values and moral compass that you operate within Motherhood.

The Boss Mom Mentality is about looking inward. Becoming self-aware is the best gift you can give to yourself, your families and can change the generational behaviors that you pass on to your children.

Self-awareness allows you the ability to quickly spot your weaknesses and make improvements. Where those whom aren't self-aware, have to go through more disappointment and heartache before learning how to improve or perhaps none at all.

You are able to show your children how to subjectively see things because you come from a place of self-awareness, which will translate in how they see themselves and their world, giving them a chance to develop inner strength and self-confidence.

Dr. Carl Jung said it best; *you are happiest when what you feel, what you think and what you say coincide with one another.* To do that, know yourself well.

There is a lot of work to do when discovering and developing who you are, but the power that becomes available to you when you know what you are working with is so rewarding. Anything of great value always takes work to achieve.

NOTES:

- Principle 9 -

Value of Emotional Resilience

Principle 9

~

Value of Emotional Resilience

"I don't measure a man's success by how high he climbs but how high he bounces back when he hits bottom."

-George S. Patton

Being able to come back from thinking negatively or feelings of disappointment took me longer than normal. I would ride my lows way too hard, in fact, there were times where I would go down the vortex of negativity, where I start counting all the things that aren't going right in my life or things that I didn't have in my life… this is all connected to my lack of emotional resilience. Do you feel like it takes you longer than normal to get out of your negative state of mind? Are there negative thoughts stewing when things don't go your way? Do you often feel like your emotions are easily moved by people or circumstances of your life?

Knowing the value of emotional resilience is key to developing your ability to bounce back from challenges that life throws at you, in this instance, the challenges that Motherhood throws your way, and this is what I need to work on for myself.

Emotional resilience is connected to how well you deal with the challenges in your life and how quickly you bounce back from them. Most whom have learned how to come back from setbacks usually get better each time a setback or challenge is presented to them, in the event that they are aware enough to learn.

Which means *resiliency* is a learned trait and you can master this skill with practice and consistency.

Why is Emotional Resilience Important to Motherhood?

There are many challenges and setbacks in the journey of Motherhood. This concept of resilience is crucial for understanding and developing because we carry the responsibility of raising our off springs.

This in turn creates strain on our inner emotional world and is a perfect breeding ground for our unhealed wounds to arise during these moments in parenting. The ability to bounce back quickly from setbacks during Motherhood is an advantage for you and the health of your emotional well-being.

Boss Mom's are able to bounce back quickly from setbacks and with practice, cultivate the ability to prevent those setbacks from reoccurring.

Define

Emotional Resilience (n)

The time you take to bounce back from any challenging moment or setback.

Do you think you have a high level of emotional resilience?

I know that I don't. I am still developing this trait, let alone having a level of resilience to it. According to Susan David, author of *Emotional Agility*; Emotions are guideposts to what is *important* and of *value* to us.

Researching this topic and reviewing the details of Emotional Agility was a huge eye-opener for me. The unemotional approach to the concept of emotional agility was un-intimidating and easy to understand. I have listed down my takeaway from her book. I encourage you to read this as well.

**Note: I will walk through how I process the negative emotion; fear and the underlying thought process connected to the emotion. As I walk you through this, I'd like for you to look at how you can assess your negative emotions and figure out what your underlying thought process is when you experience the negative emotion.

Don't Judge the Emotion

~

Often times, the moment we notice an uncomfortable emotion, we immediately go into judging the emotion and giving them meaning… which leads to allowing that emotion *power* over how we perceive the situation.

For example, if I make a mistake at work and the emotion of fear comes up for me, I notice that I judge myself for the fear I am feeling. David says, instead of judging the emotion, she says to do *nothing*.

Don't judge it and just let it be. *With time, it will pass*. This creates a space between the stimuli (in my case, fear) and my actions that follow. This concepts speak to the previous section, *"Benefits of Waiting to Respond."*

Observe the Emotion

~

Just like we notice our hands or toes, David says to notice the emotion. In my case, I would observe the emotion of fear and with time, eventually it will subside. The truth resides within the gap of your *response* to the situation and the *actual* situation.

As all emotions are temporary, it's the attention we give it that allows it any kind of power. If we can simply observe it, acknowledge it, and let it pass, that will be all the power it will have.

If we judge ourselves for our fear or frustration, or other uncomfortable emotion, we let it live that much longer and take up so much more of our day and energy than it deserves.

Examine Your Emotions to Their Roots

~

Uncover what that emotion is really about. After you've let the initial emotion subside, label the emotion for its true color. In my case, my feelings of fear are connected to not being *good enough*.

The problem resides here, like most, I notice that I start adding to the emotion of fear, my reasons as to why it is valid, making it true for me… but it's just a *false* reality that I make up.

I believe this is crucial to understand, as this is the moment where you can make a decision as to where you can take your fear and allow it to catapult you into a deeper understanding of yourself and find some resolution, or be stuck in the fear and allow it to paralyze you.

If I allow the fear to paralyze me, then it causes the same pattern it had initially, not causing for growth and empowerment. Looking beyond the face of the emotion or negative feelings allows you to see where it originated from in the first place.

"*Your greatest danger here is your ego and how it makes you unconsciously maintain illusions about yourself. These may be comforting in the moment, but in the long run they make you defensive and unable to learn or progress.*"

-Robert Greene, The Laws of Human Nature

Discover Inner Solution

~

Find a solution to bridge the gap creating the emotional understanding. Since my fear is essentially connected to "not being good enough" or "smart enough".

Think of the opposite for this to create a balance and counter the fear. The opposite of this is to remind myself of why I am worthy of my position and my accomplishments that warrant where I am at, personally or professionally. The opposite is usually the thinking of what you are thankful in this situation, accessing the concept of gratitude. Gratitude truly bridges the concept of fear and lack thereof, to being able to access feelings of abundance in each situation that creates that fear.

This kind of shift of awareness can alter my state of mind by noticing what I am thankful for and becoming grateful which turns fear into motivation and positive energy.

Journal About Your Discovery

~

"Get everything out of your head and onto paper. This frees up new energy to focus on great goals and enables you to notice and eliminate whatever is necessary and distracting. When there's lots of stuff on the mind that has nothing to do with what matters most, we lose sight the big picture."

-Robert K. Cooper, The Other 90%

I hate to bring this up so many times within the book… but its key! Journaling about your discovery is key to really allowing yourself to have these concepts sink into your mind. The act of writing things down helps the information to be stored in long term memory instead of short-term memory.

Write about the feelings that come up, dissect them one at a time and don't feel overwhelmed as this is a process of self-discovery. In fact this is a perfect opportunity to journal, if you do feel overwhelmed, write about it.

Journaling allows you to maximize the growth potential of these moments. Allow yourself to emotionally develop, which in turn create motivation for self-awareness and a step forward in a better way of living and handling the challenges of your life.

Conclusion

~

I am writing this from a place where I too have my share of insecurities and fears that plague my day to day emotional responses to my circumstances and it takes me constant work and daily awareness in how I respond. The work of self-healing is grand, and it requires commitment and honest reflection. It is in the small shifts in your behaviors and responses, that when compounded over time, create a drastic change and positive results.

The shift isn't a massive or an overwhelming task. It's small and starts in the way you think and how you observe the circumstances of your life. Cultivate a skill of knowing your level of emotional resilience and strengthening this skill, that is where the possibility resides to improve your ability to bounce back from setbacks and to start practicing this on a daily basis.

Becoming whole is accepting that we all have darkness's within us. It's the matter of bringing them to light and revealing them to yourself so that you can work through them honestly and with dignity. Work towards making these parts of yourself whole so that eventually making those fears an advantage of yours, making you more equipped to handle the challenges of life and Motherhood.

NOTES:

~ The Boss Mom Community ~

Jennel Ramos

"You can feel like you failed in life, but your children will always be your greatest accomplishment."

- Principle 10 -

Value of Adaptability

Principle 10

~

Value of Adaptability

"Overcome uncertainty at any time, by learning the skill of Adaptability.".

-M.H.

My parenting challenges are no different than anyone else's. I have trouble multitasking, getting things done while the kids are playing, I have a tendency to respond autopilot and not pay attention to my responses to my children.

I make mistakes and notice I am doing the same things as those whom have come before me. Changing these patterns takes a lot of mental awareness and that I am honestly, just too lazy to commit to 100% of the time. All the while, feeling guilty of being lazy to commit. It is a detrimental pattern, but that's why I started writing; to help me understand how to parent through sharing my experiences.

I am 5 years new into parenting and by now, I should be an expert. Given it takes 1000 hours to master a skill, if that's the case, then I've mastered this mom thing. Unfortunately, this is not a professional skill like writing contract law or becoming an engineer. The matters of the heart and raising little ones can't be mastered in 1000 hours because our children, families are ever changing.

Parenting while managing everything else is difficult and will get even harder as our children grow older and start to cultivate their own personality, beliefs and ideals. Some parents may seem like they have it figured out, but even those parents aren't fully prepared for when this happens.

Why is Adaptability Important in Motherhood?

How do you really handle the challenges within Motherhood and balancing everything else? Well, to simply put it, one must cultivate the character of Adaptability. A Boss Mom has the ability to adapt in situations, they embody a character of flexibility and can adjust when the situation calls for it.

Raising children is the toughest job in the world. It's physically demanding, emotionally exhausting, and mentally draining. Most adults aren't ready for such a task and we commonly go about doing all of this with no real plan or goals in mind.

The world of parenting is always changing, they're getting older, they are developing more of an understanding of their surroundings, whom they are as individuals and drawing their own conclusions about their world. Cultivating your ability to adapt in a given situation allows you to be steadfast in your beliefs while having the ability to mold to different situations when necessary.

Define

Adaptability (n)

Your ability to change and adapt in any given situation.

Being adaptable in all areas of life is key. Your ability to *successfully* adjust to times where your day didn't go as planned, or the results you expected didn't fruition, depends on your ability to adapt and take appropriate action when those moments take place.

Let's review some tips cultivating the skill of Adaptability in Motherhood.

Know What You Need to Do

~

This is common sense, but we all need a reminder of this even in the most common-sense times. Becoming adaptable is possessing a delicate balance of knowing what to do and how to adjust when those things that you need to do, can't be done.

As a parent and adult, you must know what you need to do on a daily, weekly and monthly basis so that your household runs smoothly, and your children are being raised and taken care of properly. Know what you need to do and how to get things done.

Be Flexible When Plans Change

~

Mistakes are inevitable, let's face it, mistakes are a part of life. In Motherhood, mistakes will happen more frequently than normal. This chapter can bring a lot of stress because of your new role and it is a time in a women's life where hormones are high, emotions are irrational, and this can affect how we handle moments within our days with our little ones.

Allow yourself room for mistakes, laugh at yourself when you do a silly mistake, figure out a way to be lighthearted about moments like this. Never beat yourself up during these moments because you are learning. Welcome the mistakes and ensure you learn from them during your journey.

Let Go of Expectations

~

Let go of expectations and you can truly have inner peace. Expecting outcomes take away from being present and truly allowing yourself to embrace and cherish your time with your children.

"*Expectations are resentments waiting to happen.*"
-Brene Brown

Truly becoming a Boss Mom is about being present and allowing yourself to feel the joys of this chapter in your life. Before you know it, your child will be at their first day of kindergarten, then middle school, then college! You will find yourself trying to recall those chubby baby moments. Enjoy them in all the different moments of their childhood and in your Motherhood and let go of expectations.

Trust the Process

~

Have you ever looked back in your life and experienced appreciation for the different lessons that each phase of your life has bestowed to you?

I have been a business owner for a short period within my early twenties… this entrepreneurship was short lived, as I wasn't mentally & emotionally capable of sustaining a successful business. A ton of lessons was learned during this phase in my life. Thanks to those lessons that I have learned over a decade ago, I can actually run and operate a successful business now.

The process of priming a person to become the person they need to be, to maintain a level of achievement, comes with process, time, a set of lessons that you must learn along the way. This same theory goes for Motherhood, you must learn how to control your emotions, during moments of high stress and respond with love.

Conclusion

~

Change is the fundamental bedrock of Parenthood. Not only in Parenthood, but in all of life, which means Adaptability is one of the aspects to cultivate to have a successful Motherhood journey.

Adaptability means possessing the quality of being flexible while parenting from a place of love and self-awareness.

Your ability to understand and develop your capabilities to bounce back quickly from situations that requires you to be flexible, become better parents, role models and problem solvers for your children.

To put it in perspective, think of new parents 50 years ago. They didn't have to worry about their child's screen time. Parents 100 years ago didn't have to worry about their teenagers learning to drive cars. Each generation of parents will face new struggles as the world constantly changes and develops. Our job as parents is to arm ourselves with resilience and knowledge so, as these changes happen, we can respond informatively and appropriately.

This applies on an even smaller level: each of our children are unique in their own way. Your first baby might be quiet, calm, and a good sleeper. Your second may be a no-sleep soldier who likes to yell. This doesn't make your second child is a bad kid, but he demands that you employ adaptability so you can raise your child from a place of love and self-awareness.

Change is inevitable. Be ready for it. Now on to the fun part of this book! Section 3!!

NOTES:

Become a Boss Mom

- Section 3-

Inner Peace & Balance

- Balancing Act
- Value of a Positive Mindset
- Value of Affirmations
- Value of Self Care
- Value of Time

Section Three

~

Inner Peace & Balance

"Self-care is giving the world the best of you, instead of the rest of you."

-Katie Reed

Section Three of The Boss Mom Mentality covers the balancing act of Motherhood and maintaining your sense of *self* & *inner* peace through the concept of Self-Care and utilizing time wisely.

Your ability to problem solve and remain calm during high stressed situations with your children directly correlates with the health of your inner world. Taking the time for yourself is absolutely imperative to being mentally healthy and well-balanced mom for your children.

The Boss Mom Mentality is about being aware of your personal worth, value and ensuring that you maintain that by taking care of yourself first.

Inner peace is the foundation where your day to day decisions and behaviors reside. Ensure that you maintain a level of inner peace to successfully show up for your children. Break away from your generational patterns of inner pain and raising your children with a negative mindset.

Instead, you call the shots, you are actively taking care of your mental health, your inner peace is untouched, thus creating a healthy Motherhood journey.

- Principle 11 -

Balancing Act

Principle 11

~

A Balancing Act

"Life is a balance between holding on and letting go."

-Rumi

After some research I've conducted on the challenge's mothers face in this ever so challenging journey, with also having the same personal issues, I've discovered that the most difficult hurdle to overcome is the concept of balancing it all and having a sense of meaning and fulfilment.

Balancing all the facets of life as a Mom can be one of the most challenging aspects. According to happyworker.com, "*72% of moms with children over the age of 1 are employed and spend an average of 13 hours of their day at an office or doing house chores.*" It is difficult and most of the time we must pick and choose what needs most of our attention in any given moment. Giving equal attention to any one person or activity is impossible, but somehow that is how most of us operate… half *assing* things and expecting things to turn out ok.

There's no two of the same days or weeks or months that we experience. As moms, our lives are ever changing, our children don't forever stay the same age, our career is always shifting, our mental and emotional stability is always in flux and our relationships with our partners can be strained from time to time.

Which means these ever so changing aspects of our lives is a constant stressor and we must be able to learn how to balance those changes. As a Boss Mom, there's usually a lot of tasks in the air when maintaining everything. I can see why some moms can go off in the deep end and some moms have longer periods of depression. The Boss Mom Mentality of Self Care is as valuable as taking care of her children. She understands the importance of self-care and how it connects with her sense of self-worth.

Let us review some valuable ways to bringing more peace and balance into your life.

Gratitude

~

The first thing about balancing Motherhood is understanding how gratitude weaves all things together. In the earlier principles I explain how gratitude allows us to bridge the gap from feelings of lack, to feelings of abundance. Being grateful, means we have the ability to recognize the good in everything. A Boss Mom has the mentality of gratitude. Having a positive attitude even during the most trying moments sounds crazy. I know, that it is easier said than done. Your ability to switch your mindset for positivity is powerful tool in your journey of Motherhood.

What I do to be grateful is to list off two or three positive things in my life that happened that day. The goal is to truly sit with the feeling of Appreciation.

For example, being able to say goodnight to my baby girls and giving them kisses before they go to sleep is a huge positive to my day.

Another grateful aspect I recognize within my days, is my ability to do everything I need to do…

Whether it be going to work, cleaning the house, making dinner, giving the girls baths and ending the night with some quality time with my man… those are great examples of what you can think of to be grateful for in your life. The simpler you make it, the easier you will find it to recognize what to be grateful for.

Whatever it is, find two or three things that went well that day for you and give it thanks and acknowledge its presence in your life.

These little shifts of attention can make the following day more positive and practices your mind to focus on the good things in your life.

Have Goal

~

"With a sense of purpose, we feel much less insecure. We have an overall sense that we are advancing, realizing some or all of our potential."

-Robert Greene, The Laws of Human Nature

The second thing about balancing Motherhood is to occupy your mind with a goal. Becoming goal oriented is putting your mind towards something positive that you want to accomplish. The Boss Mom is focused and goal oriented, not putting any attention on negativity.

As reviewed in Principle #8, if left untended, the mind can do a lot of trouble. It can start worrying and thinking negatively. Your mind is wild and can create some really bad emotions that causes detrimental behaviors and creates terrible results in your life.

The goal is to keep your mind occupied with what you're working towards and that is a goal that is valuable enough to do even during moments where you are unmotivated.

Why do you get up every morning and want to do your best and be the best version of yourself?

Think of a goal you want to achieve in your life… is it to get a promotion? Become a more present partner/mother? To finish reading a certain book. Or learn how to cook?

The good thing about goals is that, there is opportunity to shift your mind to focus on the achievement of the goal, instead of the negative things going on in your life… it redirects your attention to something more productive and increases your self awareness.

One of my goals were to write a book, about personal growth and my journey as a woman and a Mother. This has given me enlightenment and has allowed me to reflect on how to become a better person and overall has given me a level of self-confidence.

It doesn't have to be a monumental goal but have a goal to work towards, something small at first, like waking up 15 minutes early in the morning, or cutting out a sugary drink or candy bar each day to start practicing better eating habits. Then work yourself up to larger goals, like losing 10 pounds within a certain time frame.

The point is to give yourself something to work towards.

Honesty

~

Honesty gives us room to grow.

M.H.

The third aspect of balancing Motherhood is understanding honesty and how this plays in how you perceive your journey, where you are going and who you want to become. Be honest about where you are. Are you in a place of unhappiness? Do you want to make some changes in your life?

Being honest is an important Core Value and moral compass that dictate your actions and how you handle life. Being honest in all your interactions with others and including yourself creates a sense of self-worth and self-respect. Honesty goes a long way that catapult your sense of value, giving you a huge boost in self-confidence.

A Boss Mom is Honest with herself and others. Do you feel like you are lacking in some areas that you need to improve on? Discover what the opposite would look like, what would it look like if you weren't lacking, what areas in your life would be fulfilled and how would that feel?

The purpose here is to understand that we all have room for improvement and your goal should be in alignment with what you think you need improvement on.

Don’t be mean to yourself, just be honest.

Patience

~

The forth and last thing about balancing Motherhood is cultivating a sense of patience. The Boss Mom Mentality embodies patience and understands that there is a process to achieving a level of success or growth. Patience not only is about employing it with your child, or if you've told you child many times to eat his breakfast and stop playing. Patience is also on a level of accepting that any kind of growth, professionally, personally or financial growth takes time.

Don't be too hard on yourself. Go with the process of your life… be patient and don't rush results.

Define

Patience (n)

The capacity to accept or tolerate delay, trouble, or suffering without getting angry or upset.

There are seasons within our lives that prime our experiences, our emotional and mental capabilities so that when we take on larger responsibilities, so we are mentally and emotionally equipped to handle it. Trust the process, it's all happening for a reason. Often, we want results yesterday without having to put the work in.

Wouldn't it be great to lose five pounds without ever having to work up a sweat? That isn't realistic. Neither is losing five pounds overnight. A Boss Mom embodies a character of persistent effort towards her goals, not wishful thinking. It takes patience and persistence towards achieving your goals.

One of the biggest lessons I've learned in life is that you must work hard to achieve anything of great value and worth. The easy route is usually never the most stable route and lacks the potential growth you must acquire before reaching any level of success or growth.

Therefore, know that there is work involved, compounded efforts, day after day… and eventually, results can sprout. Only with a commitment to your goals, you reap what you sow.

Conclusion

~

You don't have to do it all. Just do your best!

M.H.

Balancing Motherhood is not a concept of To Do's, and what Tasks needs to get accomplished… it is a mental game. The more connected you are with yourself, the better you will be at *balancing it all.*

There is a level of becoming in Motherhood and Womanhood and takes gratitude, being focused on a goal, patience and honesty to get there. Develop your strength in this and you will be able to balance Motherhood successfully.

NOTES:

- Principle 12 -

Value of a Postive Mindset

Principle 12

~

Value of a Positive Mindset

"A pessimist sees the difficulty in every opportunity; an optimist sees the opportunity in every difficulty."

-Winston Churchill

Staying consistently positive during Motherhood is not an easy task. In fact, most may say impossible and going through bouts of emotional ups and downs is completely normal.

I mean, come on… we've birthed a child, endured physical changes to our bodies, now we come last in our lives and our needs barely get met nowadays… it's almost normal to be an emotional wreck. I get it, a Positive Mindset is the last thing you are thinking about, but studies show that those who have a positive mindset lead happier lives, achieve greater in their work or career, are in happier marriages, raise happier children and are happier people overall.

It is of importance, to figure out ways to cultivate a sense of positivity in how we perceive our world and how we parent in our children's lives.

Define

Positive Mindset (n)

A mental state that focuses on the bright side of life and expects positive results.

Having a positive mindset is key to success in your journey of Motherhood.

It's tough to stay consistently positive or motivated. Especially when we start comparing ourselves to what we believe we should be at or worse, comparing ourselves to another person's success or life.

The key maintaining a positive mindset is understanding that all feelings, including sadness, is all temporary and eventually will pass with time. Acknowledge it and let it pass... to encourage its passing, below are some tips I've used to shift my mindset, mood and overall feelings of negativity. Let's review ways to evoke a more positive viewpoint of your life, that worked for me.

Open to Possibilities

~

"It always seems impossible, until it done."

-Nelson Mandela

The magic of life is that anything is absolutely possible. Even the impossible is possible. A Boss Mom is open to all possibilities.

Logic can get in the way of using your imagination and being open to the possibilities of what could be. Be rational while also knowing that the magic of life, can truly create the impossible to be possible.

The Universe always conspires towards what you strongly believe in. According to Deepak Chopra in *The Seven Laws of Spiritual Success;* on creating affluence, he says "*You have the ability to acquire anything that falls within the realm of your imagination.*"

Exercise

~

It's a no brainer that exercise does the body good, but it is also proven to improve your mental state and overall create a happier you. Blood flow and increased endorphins create a series of chemicals that promote happiness and peace. Endorphins are so powerful that their chemical reaction on the brain is similar to that of morphine! How's that for natural medicine?

If it's been some time since you've exercised, then do something easy like a brisk walk or yoga stretches at first. There's no need to go out and run a marathon when a stroll around the block will do. You don't need to be an expert. As long as you get some blood flow going, you're on the right track.

Exercise at least 3-4 times a week, 10 minutes of working out makes a big difference in shifting your mindset to become happier, more productive and a healthy mommy. Increase your workout time as you build endurance and strength.

A gym membership may be fun and motivating to some, but there is also no need to spend money if you don't have the means. There are many free online exercise resources to follow that range from beginner to expert levels. Look up YouTube tutorials or even Instagram fitness pages for motivation!

Gratitude

~

Gratitude is the healthiest of all human emotion.

-Zig Ziglar

Gratitude is literally the key of all… so listing this concept more than once is needed to make a point. Having a mindset of gratitude is hard if you are not used to thinking this way or if you're naturally pessimistic. Being aware of what you are thankful for helps with understanding what positive things to focus on in your life.

Even though you may naturally be a glass half empty type of person, you can learn to think positively. By giving attention to what you are grateful for, you can create more of that specific positive thing in your life.

It's simple: thinking of more lack... the universe will give you more lack. Vice versa, thinking of more abundance, more gratitude of things you already possess, the universe will give you more of these positive feelings in your life.

Gratitude Exercise

~

On a daily basis, think about at least three things you're grateful for. Once in the morning and once in the evening before bed. Even the smallest things like a hot cup of coffee or a sunny day counts!

List 3 Things That You Are Grateful For

1. ____________________________

2. ____________________________

3. ____________________________

~~

The purpose of this exercise is to get you thinking about what you are grateful for. Placing your attention on the things that you are happy about creates happy chemicals in the brain that decrease stress hormones and allows you to focus on the positivity in your life.

According to Dr. Wayne Dyer, "*gratitude is the gateway to manifesting the life you want*". This kind of awareness shift will promote an increase of blessings, love and overall happiness in your life.

Like Minded People

~

You can't hang out with negative people and expect to live a positive life.

-Joel Olsteen

Strong women roll with other strong women whom share similar Principles and Core Values. Changing your habits is hard. It's even more difficult if you're surrounded with people who practice those old habits.

The saying "*You are who you hang out with,*" is reality. If you are with positive people, you will start thinking positively.

If you are around lazy or negative people, you will start becoming like this. Your actions will be affected, and you will start embodying their actions.

"The human mind is a form of energy, a part of it being spiritual in nature. When the minds of two people are coordinated in a spirit of harmony, the spiritual unit of the energy of each mind form an affinity, which constitutes the "Psychic" phase of the Mastermind."

-Napoleon Hill, *Think & Grow Rich.*

Watch out for the people you spend the most time with as it is a reflection of who you are, where you will be and the kind of results you get.

Get Rest

~

Getting rest is a no brainer, but surprisingly, many people including moms, especially new moms, will find themselves operating with a very small amount of sleep. As part to operating in mindful way, and being present in your Motherhood journey, sleep is a necessity.

Did you know sleep supports the brain and how we respond in our lives? Ahead, I've dedicated a whole chapter on the concept of Self Care. A person is not able to positively give from an empty cup.

Becoming a Boss Mom encompasses many things of self-discovery & an aspect of that is, Self-Care. Self-care includes, getting rest, get some shut eye and take a break from your household.

Ask family members or close friends to help you with watching the kids for a couple of hours.

Get some you time, to feel normal and to practice self-love and worth. Ask your support system to help you with this. Just for a small part of your day. Your chance to take care of yourself and fill your cup up is crucial.

Conclusion

~

"We are what we think, all that we are arises with our thoughts. With our thoughts, we make the world."

-Buddha

It is difficult to cultivate a positive mindset, when all you've been used to is negative outcomes that seem to continue within your life. This is the essential root of where those negative outcomes are derived from… being used to it, expecting it, making it your ultimate reality.

Instead, try a different outcome, get used to a more positive outcome, even if, at first it is foreign to you. Naturally, it will be foreign… but if you embody and adopt a new mindset, a positive mindset… you may get something different in your life.

Becoming aware and accepting that it's okay to feel sad or down is the first step to shifting your overall mindset. Accept that this is a part of being alive and being a mother. You will experience ups and downs of life, don't judge yourself for it, it is what it is, and this will pass with time. It's the matter of knowing how to change it and what to do when you get in a funk. These feelings are normal, don't judge yourself for it, just do something about it.

NOTES:

~ The Boss Mom Community ~

Jerlyn Gabaon

"In the midst of Motherhood, work, & life— I am reawakened knowing he is the beat of my heart, the pulse in my vein, and reason of strength.

My son is the energy to my soul. Never neglect time with your children for in the chaos of it all, time is love."

- Principle 13 -

Value of Affirmations

Principle 13

~

Value of Affirmations

"What we think, we become."

-Buddha

Do you ever take the time to think about what kinds of thoughts are living behind your parenting skills or how you show up in your household or life? Do you take an active role in how you parent your children or how you show up in their lives? Are you present in your child's life or are you letting others raise them?

In a very true and interesting way, the answers to these questions, make an impact on any parent, subconsciously. The way you show up in your life, whether good or bad, is all connected to what you tell yourself, your inner dialogue or mental chatter... these are called affirmations.

To improve your mindset within parenting and life, harnessing the power of affirmations is extremely powerful. Having impactful affirmations to tell yourself daily is what can change your overall belief of yourself, your life and the circumstances within it. Feeding your mind fruitful thoughts that help you stay focused, organized and have a clear goal in your Motherhood journey will affect your behavior, your actions, it creates empowerment and builds your self-confidence.

Define

Affirmations (n)

The action or process of affirming something or being affirmed.

Affirmations is about creating a personal statement that promotes a positive mindset which should be repeated to your self and written frequently.

About fifteen years ago, I first learned about the power of Affirmations from the great Louise Hay, Author of *Heal Your Life*. Haye have been teaching the power of affirmations for over 25 years.

She has used affirmations to heal herself of cancer, heal from abuse and to transform her life into great success and prosperity. Haye defines affirmations as, "*every thought we think, every word we speak to be an affirmation that transforms our lives.*"

Why are Affirmations Important in Motherhood?

"I know that effective thinking-thinking can alter self-destructive behavior-does not occur just because something is said. An insight must be repeated, and repeated, repeated again. Only then, when it is fully accepted and understood, do you begin to alter behavior."

-Dr. Wayne Dyer, Your Erroneous Zones

Being able to take control of your Motherhood journey through affirmations is a powerful and very easy tool you can start doing now, literally… right now. Louise Hay shares the experiences of having a mindset of love, positivity and praying with intent to manifest a life that you really want through affirmations and be conscious of the words that you say to yourself.

Affirmations are a great way to keep yourself centered within the hustle and bustle of life and to get out of the default thinking of the negativity and sacrifice.

Detrimental Loop vs. Instrumental Loop

~

Have you ever experienced someone close to you that seem to be going through the same problems over and over again?

I know someone real close to me, whom seem to just have a very strong Detrimental Loop. I call this a loop, because it keeps happening to her, the same problem over and over again.

In Dr. Wayne Dyer's book, *A Spiritual Solution to Every Problem*, he talks about having a spiritual solution to every problem, literally. For my dear friend whom seem to be encountering the same problem over and over again, there's something spiritual she needs to learn, for it to actually stop happening to her.

The problem? She operates from a sense of lack, not having enough, not having her needs met one way or another, she possesses a strong emotion of *needing* and *not having*. She has a terrible relationship with money; when she has money, she blows it on things that aren't a priority. When she doesn't have it, she complains that she has no money and focuses on lack. Either way, whether she has money or doesn't, she focuses on lack. Thus, giving her the same experience… lack, not having enough and a sense of *wanting*.

I coined the term; ***Detrimental Loop*** to represent the negative thought process that keeps giving you results that aren't benefiting you or your life. These negative processes will keep going on if left unnoticed or unchanged. Affirmations are a great way to change your Detrimental Loop and replace it with an Instrumental Loop.

An ***Instrumental Loop*** represents a positive thought process that benefits your life and helps you achieve your goals. You can cultivate an Instrumental Loop thought process through the practice of Affirmations.

These statements are a great way to keep yourself out of the detrimental loop that we tend to perpetuate within our lives if we don't take control of our responses and reactions towards people and this case our children or feelings of Motherhood.

Motherhood Affirmations can be used to remind you of what's important during trying and emotional moments.

Below is my list of Motherhood Affirmations that help keep me aligned with parenting positively, purposefully and compassionately.

Boss Mom Affirmations

~

1. I am a present mother.
2. I am in tune with my children's needs.
3. I am a positive role model for my children.
4. I have flourishing relationships with my children.
5. My children are healthy and happy.
6. I have a strong connection with my child.
7. I am a conscious parent.
8. I exercise compassion while teaching my children tough lessons.
9. I am a fair parent.
10. I am a loving parent.

Those are my examples of affirmations in my own life. I am not a 100% perfect, nor am I trying to be. What I am trying to do is parent better and take the time to think about my actions and how I respond to my children and the circumstances of my life. The way I do this is to be conscious of my thoughts and affirmations is a tool to shift my mindset to focus.

I encourage you to journal about what your parenting goals are, then create your own affirmations that help you stay aligned with your goals.

The list above is to help create your own affirmations, give you insight on how each affirmation should be formatted and you can tweak my affirmations and gear them to you and your Motherhood style.

Start it with "*I am*" … follow it with something you want to see in your life, example:

I am a Powerful Woman.

If you don't have a journal to write in, I encourage you to purchase a notebook. Within your notebook write your thoughts, affirmations, goals of parenthood and help keep your mind clear and focused.

NOTES:

"Repetition of affirmation of orders to your subconscious mind is the only known method of voluntary development of the motion of faith."

-Napoleon Hill, *Think & Grow Rich*

- Principle 14 -

Value of Self Care

Principle 14

~

Value of Self-Care

You cannot give from an empty cup.

-M.H.

I am a career woman by day, Mommy of two and wife by night, podcaster & author when all have gone to bed and in between. I notice that I can get a bit crazy, over-emotional, and stressed if things don't go the way that I planned or, even worse, a grumpy momma to my kids. Modern Day Motherhood includes a lot of responsibilities, we have gotten busier and busier as the decades progressed.

One of which is being a side hustler. I know moms whom write books on the side of their day jobs, hustle makeup, life insurance or diet supplements, you name it, all to make a better living for themselves and their families.

It's a lot, I know!

The one thing I do know is to not compromise my happiness and wellbeing for anything that can wait. A lot of us strive for perfection. We have to make sure the laundry is all done, folded, pressed and put away, ensure that all the dishes are washed and dried, be sure to clean the entire house from top to bottom and the list goes on and on.

In reality, all those things can wait. The Boss Mom Mentality is nurtured through Self-Care and there is no rush to get everything completed, especially if it compromises your time to relax and woosah at the end of your day.

If you are getting too cranky because it's time for you to relax, do it and stop doing stuff that can wait. Allow yourself time to mentally, emotionally and physically regroup, even for 10-15 minutes at the end of your day. During the course of this journey, I have learned something that helped me realize my priorities:

Time is sacred, and perfection is unrealistic.

Having *Me Time* is sacred to the way I talk to my children, the way I respond to my partner and the overall atmosphere of my household. Moms have a powerful energy that we exude and must keep sacred and nurtured. Otherwise we are doomed to raising unhappy children and in an unhappy marriage.

Let's visit some cheap and easy things to do at home that encourage some inner peace, restore your self-worth and decompress.

Note: Dad or a sitter needs to be enlisted to help with looking after the kids or you can do these below after everyone's gone to bed!

Soak in a Bath

~

Taking a bath after a long day of work and managing your household is the best feeling.

Baths immediately put you in a tranquil state and promote overall stress relieving chemicals. I usually add Epsom Salt to my bath for the qualities within the salt promotes amazing healing results to the body.

Baths allow you to reflect on what you are grateful for. How your day went, what you could improve on, what activities to do with your children for the following day or weekend. You can give yourself the space to critically think about problems and help with coming up with solutions.

Aside from the mental benefits, a nice hot soak does wonders for those sore mommy muscles and aching feet from chasing little ones all day. Treat yourself to a bath and a glass of wine as needed!

Foot Soak

~

This is my ultimate favorite, a good foot soak. Just like above, I use Epsom salt and add an extra antibacterial agent: tea tree oil. It smells amazing and it's easier to do than a whole bath.

Grab a bucket that you can soak your feet in, fill it tall enough to your ankles with hot/warm water so that it doesn't cool down too fast. I usually do this before bed, that way it helps with removing callous build up. Soaking my feet in this, makes my problems and stresses melt away!

Face Mask

~

Making time for face masks is one of the best ways you can take care of your skin. I am in my early thirties and notice that my skin is not how it used to be 10 years ago.

I have to take the time to take care of it, like getting the right products to use and actually take the time to do it. Long gone are the days of falling asleep with make up on!

Face masks are one of the items I use once a week to make me feel good about myself and promote self-care and most importantly, to take care of my skin. When my skin looks good, I feel good.

This activity is considered anti-aging and can help your skin stay supple, promote cellular turnover and lessens the appearance of lines. You are not only taking care of yourself mentally by doing face masks, but you are also taking care of your skin! It's your biggest organ-take care of it!

Reflection

~

Can you tell I encourage journaling yet? I've gone into detail about this in Section Two and the benefits of journaling. I've found that this is the best mental decompressing activity that helps release stress, solve problems and help gain some insight into our chaos-filled minds.

Get a journal and a pen and start writing. Write about anything: about your day, what were its *high's* and it's *low's*. You will be surprised with what comes out. It's my form of therapy, it helps with understanding situations, inspiring thoughtful action for better results and promotes goal achievement.

The physical act of writing your goals down, activates the Prefrontal Lobe in your brain where thinking and cognition take place. During your day to day activities, ideas sprout because you've planted a seed of your goal within your mind. I've gone into detail on how the brain is affected when you journal, in Principle #6. The subconscious mind is always listening and is listening, even more, when you write down your thoughts.

Conclusion

~

Making time for yourself is key to being able to love, nurture and care for the people dearest to you. Motherhood is an invaluable journey that will test us, prepare us and mold us into the woman for our children where they will learn from. Be sure to be in a state of positivity during this journey. You can't give anything positive, if you are giving from an empty cup. Fill yourself up with love and self-care, allow yourself sometime to restore your grace and regain a level of self-love.

Our children see us as role models, be a role model to them that you can be proud of and take the time to get yourself centered on a more frequent basis so that you are able to be a present and loving parent and partner.

NOTES:

~ The Boss Mom Community ~

Candice B.

"Find your balance. Set time for family, career, friends and yourself. Time flies and you can't take it back, so don't take time for granted.

Us moms get really busy with our work or career, cooking, cleaning, making doctor appointments. you name it. We need to make sure we dedicate time for our family and friends: your partner, your kids (they grow up so fast). Call them while at work at lunch time or just anytime just to say hi, or text, say that you love them when you're not with them.

Call a friend when you're on a train getting home just to say hi and see how they're doing. Call your mom, visit your parents. It seems so much, but really, you just have to make time to do it. Last, but not least, take time for yourself. Listen to music with your headphones or go to a quiet place close your eyes, relax and reflect. Even if you're just in your car alone for 5 min before you enter your home.

- Principle 15 -

Value of Time

Principle 15

~

Value of Time

"Don't count the days, make the days count."

-Muhammad Ali

Thank god for social media and technology, because without it I wouldn't have all the amazing memories captured from my children's first baths, or first steps, or first time at Disneyland. My daughters are 3 and 5 years old and I find myself scrolling down my Instagram photos and searching for some very old content of my little ones.

It seems as though in one moment, you are kissing the chubby cheeks of your baby, then you blink, and your baby is a toddler. A moment later, they are going to school and the next they're learning to drive. Motherhood has a unique way of making time go by faster.

Embracing the moments of their childhood is the only way we can truly be present and allow for us to truly cherish these moments. Don't let the little pettiness of the day to day rob you of your joyous time with your children. The most valuable commodity in life is *time*, utilize it wisely to benefit your life and maximize each moment within it.

Let's visit some interesting insights on how you can cultivate appreciation and implement some ways to use your time effectively and change the negative mindset you have towards time, feeling like you're spread thin and feelings of not having enough time in the day.

Grudges, a Thief of Time

~

Do you ever find yourself feeling angry? We all feel anger sometimes. It's a normal and a healthy emotion, but grudges are not healthy. Grudges take your anger and makes it bleed into days and weeks tainting all of your positive moments.

Let yourself be angry when you're angry and let it go. Do whatever you need to do to release the emotion. Journal about it, meditate on it, vent to your best friend or take a walk.

Your child doesn't deserve your anger or negativity, heck no one does. Don't let angry words at a birthday party or a slight from a friend or relative cloud your days. When you allow anger or other negative emotions rule your life, it seeps into all other parts.

It can make you bitter and irritable. Your child, undeservingly, will get the brunt of it if left unresolved. If you let bitterness in, the small, joyous moments will be tainted or forgotten. It's okay to be angry. It's not okay to let anger rule your life and ruin your joy.

Don't Sweat the Small Stuff

~

Maybe it's been a hectic day and you had to eat take-out for lunch, or your baby spent more hours than you meant them to with a babysitter.

Whatever it is that makes you feel negative, acknowledge it and then move on. The day ends and tomorrow is a fresh start.

Sometimes the little things will get in the way and you'll get in a funk, but at the end of the day, it's over and you can snuggle your little one and try again tomorrow. Time passes way too quickly to get caught up in the small mishaps of daily life.

Small inconveniences and mistakes are what give life flavor. If you get caught up in them or allow them to ruin your whole day, you'll lose days of your life to things that won't matter even hours after they happen.

Enjoy the Little Moments

~

It's okay to not feel good about the baby spitting up on you for the fourth time that day. It's okay to not be thrilled that you haven't had a proper shower in three days and it's okay to feel tired and overwhelmed. If you're feeling seriously overwhelmed or depressed, always seek professional help like I stated in the beginning of this book!

It's easy to feel resentful when a woman in the grocery store tells you that it goes by so fast and to enjoy it when your toddler is having a meltdown in the cereal aisle, but the reality is that it really does go by so fast. Someday, you'll miss the baby coos and the sticky toddler fingers.

Someday you'll look back and might not remember the details of the extravagant birthday party you threw or the family reunion where you got to introduce your little one to your extended family.

However, you will remember their first steps, their first word, the first time they tried spaghetti. You'll remember the messes and the late nights and early mornings, how tired you were and how overwhelmed you were, but you'll also remember that you were a new mom with a beautiful new baby. You'll look back at how far you both have come and wish it hadn't flown by so quickly.

It's not the big parties or the events or vacations that make up the big picture. One day, all too soon, your child will be grown, and they won't remember the big things, but the simple moments that made them feel special.

Don't get caught up in the big events or showy displays. Be in the moment because they're what make up a lifetime of memories for you and your family. Our children grow up impossibly fast.

Your children are only small once, practice being in the moment and treasure the good and bad times. Don’t waste that precious time in anger or distraction. We’ll look forward to getting to know them as they grow but we’ll always miss how little they were.

Death of All Achievement

~

The opposite of valuing time is that paralyzing word ... ***procrastination***. The death of all achievement is in short, procrastination.

By definition, to procrastinate, is to delay or postpone action or put off doing something.

Procrastination is the death of great things in motion. Even when it comes to accomplishing anything great like, developing self-awareness, improving your parenting skills or achieving any kind of goals you have set. Are you a victim of procrastination?

There is a level of self-worth that is connected to why someone procrastinates. Within my journey of Personal Development and growth, I noticed that your level of self-worth is one way or another connected to your level of ability to complete a task.

In a sense, it is connected to how that person sees the value of completing the task. For example, if you want to lose 10 pounds, you will need to back up the goal with actions, like going to the gym or doing home exercises and eating healthy.

If the person, doesn't see the value in losing weight and getting in shape, and would rather be comfortable sitting on the couch, scrolling through their timeline or watching TV then you will see that the person will not go to the gym or eat healthy.

Procrastination is all connected to your personal value of the goal, and the level of your self-worth of achieving that goal… do you feel worthy enough to lose 10 pounds? I saw a quote, it said; "*What you eat, shows your level of your self-respect.*"

If someone feels worthy of a healthy body, to look and feel good and they found that important to maintain, they will make a conscious decision to eat healthy, start exercising or participating in activities that promotes a healthy lifestyle.

People complain about not having enough time, but it is all due to poor time management, rather they procrastinate and not actually work on the goal they ultimate want to achieve. The importance of using your time wisely and eliminating procrastination in Motherhood in order to make the necessary behavioral and emotional changes can get us on the track of true inner growth, personal discovery and mindful parenting.

Task Oriented

~

The value of time is about being Task Oriented, which is the opposite of Procrastination. Task Oriented is not about only having a bunch of your tasks on your To Do List… it is about having a To Do List that is production based and being focused on what you need to get done within your day and to achieve a goal that you have.

What is a Production Based To Do List?

This is a list of things that you need to do within your business or work, that is lead generating, or income generating. A lot of times, people spend their time on admin work or scrolling through social media or online shopping, when you could have been doing *production based tasked.* So when the time comes to spend with your family, you are not *half assing* it and you are fully present. This is called, using your time wisely!

There is a reason why those whom achieve highly, are task oriented and production based. To achieve greatness, like a health goal or completing a big project, there are little things that consistently need to be completed to achieve that end goal.

The daily habits that we do on a consistent basis is what makes up our days, weeks and the results of the year, and decade, and at the end of it all….the results of our lives.

The tasks we participate in on a daily basis constitute the successes we have in life or lack thereof.

When we show our children that there is success in being Tasked Oriented, they will be that within their own lives.

People underestimate what you can accomplish in 1 year, or 2 years or 5 years… society has programed you to want results right away. When it is the opposite of what you should be doing… which is working now for the results you want in the future.

You must figure out the end goal and work daily towards that goal, so you can actually look back at your life and say, YES! I have accomplished doing this, or have achieved that, or have done this with my life.

Becoming aware of my daily habits was a huge eye opener for me. My biggest goal was to become a successfully writer/author, my entire life, I have always wanted to write. My goal this year was to complete a book by end of summer and start on my Volume 2. It took me having to write on a daily basis, actively researching my topic, constantly looking for inspiration in all aspects of my life and carving out time in every available minute of my day.

That is the sacrifice you make when you see that your goal is that valuable to you. Become task oriented and get it done.

Teach your children to do their homework first, or complete their chores… then their reward is a snack or toys. This creates for highly productive children.

A *Meaningful* To Do List

~

Within the Value of Time and being present is creating for yourself a Meaningful To Do list. Do you currently have a daily or weekly To Do list?

I do it is filled with day to day duties like making important appointments or pay a certain bill or complete a certain project. I noticed that my To Do Lists are never something truly *meaningful*, like creating connection with my partner or stay present with my children when we play or reading to my girls right before bed.

A meaningful To Do list is exactly that, to create a *meaningful* To Do list. One that creates experiences, memorable experiences with whom you cherish the most. There is a delicate balance of being task oriented to being Connection Oriented.

Create more moments where you are creating connection, love and fun with those whom you love the most. Don't stay busy on your devices or tv or stuck in your day to day life. Truly get out of your head and love up on your peeps and create a meaningful To Do list!

Create Routines

~

The main topic of this final section is utilizing your time wisely so that you can be fully present with your loved ones. I am guilty of thinking of other things like tasks I need to get done or respond to clients but creating routines helped minimize my lack of presence in each moment with my children. One of the things you can do to save time is to *create routines.*

The more you implement routines in your life, the more time you have to focus on important things life spending quality time with your families, being more present with your children and partner or more time for yourself.

Routines help with putting into place systems that aid with streamlining your day to day duties. Streamlining your day to day can help with saving time and having items on autopilot which can lead to a less stressful day.

Let us review some ways you can create routines in your mom life, that worked for me.

Morning Routine

~

A successful morning routine is what I started putting into place because I've found that I used my time more wisely. As I start my day, I am not frazzled and rushing in the morning and it gives me a sense of self-confidence because I am prepared walking into my day.

For moms, it is difficult to remember everything before leaving for work in the morning or if you have busy day ahead. The goal is to get a system going so that you can start relaxing more after you've put your system in place. Efficiency comes with planning and systems, having routines will help you stay organized and accomplish your goal.

AM Routine

1| Prepare the Night Before

Preparing the night before and having a night regimen is key to a successful and productive morning.

Get your outfit ready in your closet, get your keys where they can easily be grabbed on your way out, prepare your coffee and have it on a timer so it can brew according to the time you wake.

Prepare the things that you will need the night before. The last thing you want is you running around the house trying to find your keys, or you miss your morning coffee because you didn't allow yourself time to brew a fresh pot.

2| Set your Alarm 15 Minutes Earlier

If you usually wake up at 630am, set your alarm to go off at 615am. When the alarm goes off, get up.

This extra 15 minutes is heaven in the morning. This will help you with getting extra time to watch the news, clean up, organize your schedule for the day or plan your drive and possible traffic in the morning.

Better to have extra time, then running late and being frazzled.

3| Drink Glass of Water

Right when you wake up, drink a glass of water. Drinking a glass of water activates all of your organs and your metabolism.

Did you know that your body loses a liter of water when you're sleeping for an 8-hour time frame? Replenish your body and wake-up your senses and organs by drinking a glass of water. This also helps with starting up your metabolism.

4| Eat Breakfast

Eat a high a protein breakfast. This will give you energy through lunch and starts your metabolism. Studies show that those whom eat a healthy breakfast tend to be more fit and lean then those who don't.

Eating a healthy breakfast is a great way to wake the body up, break your fast and start your day.

5| Get to Work at the Same Time Each Day

Allow yourself time to get to work, prepare for any kind traffic or if you happen to forget something you can make a quick U turn and get it at home. If you don't give yourself time for these little mishaps, you will definitely be late.

I like to watch the news before I go to work, the news will go over the travel time on the main highways, this usually gives me an insight on what the traffic may look like on my drive into the office.

Our smart phones are so savvy now that Google Maps will send you alerts on your travel time to destinations that you frequent like home or your office.

Evening Routine

~

A peaceful evening routine will help you with winding down your day, getting more peace and allowing you take it down in a balanced, organized and purposeful fashion. An evening routine can be made specific to you and your family needs.

The goal is to get some sort of system going so that you can start relaxing more after you've put your system in place. Efficiency comes with planning, systems and having routines will help you stay organized and accomplish your goals. In this case, your goal is to have a peaceful and purposeful evening.

Let's visit some general ways to implement a Peaceful Evening Routine that helped me and my family.

PM Routine

1| Sleep Schedule

Get your family on a sleeping schedule. This is a routine in itself, I have taught my children that by 9pm, it is their bedtime. Baths, teeth brushed, jammies on and we do a Grateful Prayer.

I try to sleep at the same time each night. As long as I get about 6 or more hours of sleep, I am good to go.

2| Prepare Attire

Plan out your children's clothes along with what you will be wearing for the next day.

The point of this is that you have everything you need ready, to prevent mishap of choosing the wrong pair of socks or not finding that blouse you planned on wearing that morning.

I am guilty of arriving to work not feeling good about what I have on, because I didn't plant ahead of time.

3| Get Breakfast & Coffee Ready

It is recommended that you have breakfast in the morning, it is the most important meal of the day, because it breaks your fast, gets your organs fired up and turns on your metabolism.

Get your coffee prepared, either on a timer or ready to be brewed in the morning.

Get your breakfast snacks ready and out.

4| Review Your Itinerary

It is always key to review your itinerary, look at what you will be doing for the following day. Organizing your appointments, who you will be meeting, doctors' visits, school activities/appointments etc.

Know what your day looks like so you can plan for this ahead of time and know ahead of time on where you are driving to.

5| Set Your Alarm 15 Minutes Early

I list this twice because this is crucial. Having that extra 15 minutes of time in the morning is key to being prepared for any traffic mishap, or a morning tantrum from a child, or a tire flat.

A 15-minute window will help you solve the situation before you can be late for work or an appointment.

6| Grateful Prayer or Nightly Affirmation

According to the Secrets of the Ages, by Robert Collier; *"Psychologist have discovered that the best time to make suggestions to your subconscious mind is just before going to sleep, when the senses are quiet, and the body is relaxed."*

I do a grateful prayer with my kids. For me, I do this throughout my day, but introducing this concept to my children seemed to make sense to do at night. Right before bed, I ask them what they are grateful for.

It's simple, they tell me a few things they are happy about that happened that day. This helps with creating a positive mindset, set your mind to focus on positivity in your day.

For my children, it allows them to learn there is always something to be grateful for.

I equate a grateful prayer as supportive affirmations before going to bed. State to yourself affirmations that help attract it in your life more of the blessings you already have and thank the universe for the amazing people, things an experience in your life.

Grateful Prayer Statements

"I am thankful for my day with my kids"

"I am thankful for my house, my car and my job"

"I am thankful for my healthy and happy family."

~~

You can come up with your own that are more specific to you and your family.

Developing a deep appreciate for the people places and things in your life and cultivating an attitude of gratitude creates more of it.

The more grateful you are, the more those grateful things continue to show up in your life, it's literally that easy.

7| Adequate Rest

The minimum amount of sleep any person should have nightly is between 6-8 hours of sleep on an average.

Rest is important for the body to reenergize; it also helps the health of your brain. During sleep, your brain is converting short term memory to long term memory. Which is important for mental cognition, reasoning, memory and overall health of your brain.

The amount of sleep that a person requires to feel fully rested for the next day, differs from each person. By now, you should know what the amount of sleep that you require to feel rested well enough to be alert and present for the next day.

I can operate well off of 6 hours of sleep. Anything less than this, I will be groggy or too sleepy to focus. Get the amount of sleep that your body requires so that you are well rested and have energy for your day.

Be Present

~

One of the hardest things in Motherhood is to allow myself to be fully present with my children.

There are so many distractions with television, cell phones and the drama of life. Those distractions take away from the precious moment with you children, family and being present.

James Gimian the publisher or Mindful.org has illustrated a way for people to weave mindfulness in all things that we do while in the grind of our daily lives.

A.R.T. is so helpful with reminding myself to be present in different parts of my day.

The amazing thing about this concept is that you can easily remember it as it represents the following:

A - Activities. Bring mindfulness in **activities** you love to do.

R - Routines. Choose one **routine** to bring mindfulness in.

T-Triggers. One of the things that are hot buttons or **triggers**, choose mindfulness instead of reacting negatively.

Below is the illustration by Gimian:

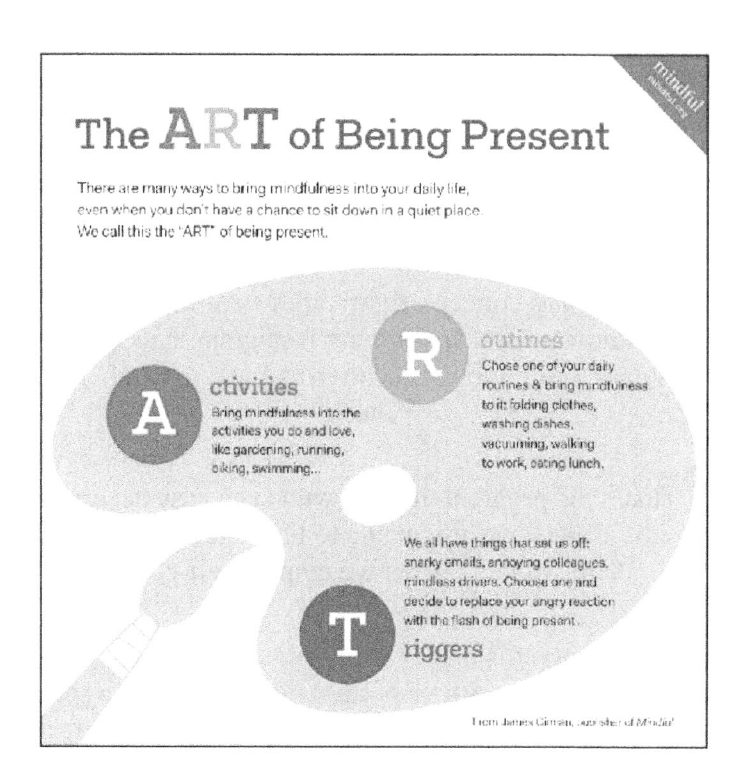

This a good reminder of how to be Present during your moments of day to day in Motherhood.

How to Be Present

~

1| Put Away Devices

This is hard concept, right? I felt so at first!! I want to know what's up with my Instagram, Facebook, emails and Pinterest, as often as I can remember to check!

That's the problem though, with such easy access to these sites, we are unable to limit ourselves from them… that is when we employ self-control.

Self-control is one of the key points here. For you to be present with your child, you will need to see the value in doing so and develop some self-control to put your devices away.

Have your device charging for the next hour or so, tell yourself it needs some juice.

2| Carve Out Time for You

Time for yourself is what will allow you to be fully "being present". For me, waking up a couple of hours before my toddlers wake up is key.

It allows me to get myself ready, get my coffee, do some writing, get my posts ready, do some before cleaning and allows me to get into the third section.

3| Plan Out the Day

Mentally prepare yourself and start off your morning with some *you time*. Plan out your toddler's morning, then commit to being fully present during breakfast.

Plan a portion of your time to clean, let your toddlers know exactly what they should be expecting, *"Mommy is going to clean the kitchen, for now you can watch Mickey Mouse."*

That way, your toddler is clear that Mommy is doing something right now, it doesn't blur the lines of Mommy and Me time.

When you're done, commit to being fully present with your child, give yourself a reasonable timeframe, have fun and connect with your child. Plan some afternoon activities, like gardening with Mommy, do some fun arts and crafts at the dining table, play some card games, do letters and numbers.

4| Complete Your Tasks

Once you've planned your day, now it's the matter of completing your tasks on your schedule. Completing the tasks you set, will help you to become present in your life… at the end of your day, you devote present time with your loved ones with no guilt of incomplete tasks.

Conclusion

~

The Value of Time was probably the hardest to write about as this concept to me has been fleeting, the older my children get, the less time I seem to have with them. I understand that this is all in my head. The fixer to this is to become *present* in the moments I share with my family, savor their hugs, kisses and quirky statements that reveal their funny and intellectual personalities.

I daydream about whom they will become when they get older, one perhaps being a writer like me… imaginative, carefree and ambitious, while the other, an intellectual, with an uncanny way of seeing life beyond her time. Being present in all moments in my life, especially in motherhood, can be the hardest task… even n the concept of daydreaming about my future, I am not being present. It is easier said than done…with each day passing, they are getting older and so am I. Before I know it, they will be in high school wondering about their prom dress… or what college to go.

I want to end this with the concept that *time* is just a measurable tool to scale the moments in our lives and this is the only thing we can leverage to maximize the days. You can get everything done in your day as long you use your time wisely. Then, you can truly devote the rest of our non-working day with those whom you cherish the most… all of this is done by putting systems and routines in place to becoming fully *present*in this truly rewarding journey of Motherhood.

NOTES:

~ The Boss Mom Community ~

Meg Calvin

"For those moms wanting to up their presence with those that they love and their productivity in the work that they love, it's all about your tools, your level of trust and how you view time.

***TOOLS:** ApDetox Ap helps me find margin with using my phone. Insight Timer Ap helps to make meditating easy. Planoly helps me schedule out my social media marketing.*

***TRUST:** Trust yourself, trust your child, trust others to take care of you and help you to care for your child.*

***TIME:** All we have is now. The secret to innovation is to stay present and to stay curious. If you are struggling to stay present, whether at home or at work, simply tap into your senses and ask a question."*

Final Notes

~

"The man who masters himself is delivered from the force that binds all creatures."

-Johann Wolfgang con Goethe

I was raised by a single mom, whom travelled to the states from the Philippines, while she was in her final trimester with me along with two teenage old sisters. My mom is resilient and raised me the best she knew how. However, I have learned her generational pains, as she raised me with her unhealed heart. Now, I carry that weight of emotional imbalance and heartache in my own life.

As a mom to two little girls, I realize the work I have ahead of me to be sure that I don't pass on debilitating thought processes on to them. It's hard at times and it takes consistence and self-awareness to be effective.

My inspiration for writing this book came from many things; my passion for Personal Development and Self Improvement, and my passion for raising my children in the healthiest state of mind that I can embody. The Boss Mom Mentality is the best way to describe what I stand for and what I try to embody on a daily basis. Don't get me wrong, I am still human, there are days that I want to slack off, but more often time, I am trying my best.

If you've read this book from cover to cover, congratulations to you! *First*, because I am a terrible writer but my passion for this superseded my personally self-imposed talent of writing. I applaud you for going through the grueling paragraphs and hope that you've received value. *Second*, because this is a sign of how serious you are at improving your personal skills to become better moms for your children and cultivating The Boss Mom Mentality.

I've presented two questions in the beginning of this book and now that you're at the end… what are your answers?

What can I learn from in these moments of Motherhood?

How do I access my inner Boss Mom?

If you have a journal, write it out, answer those questions for yourself. Personal Development is a journey that requires honesty and commitment. For that, I honor you for your bravery in this very honest journey!

Acknowledgements

~

To my better half, the best father to my children and the partner in my life. Jourdan, thank you for your constant unwavering support, your commitment to our family and the rock that you have been to us through the years.

The two that blessed me to become a Mother, Aaliyah & Sophia, whom are constantly teaching me on a daily basis. You both are constantly reminding me that I have much more to learn about, as an individual, woman and Mother. You are my world, forever… even when you've grown. I will always be here for the both of you, I dedicate this book to the both of you.

To the women whom helped shape the person I am today, my two sisters and my sweet mom, I thank you and love you.

About the Author

~

Maria Henderson is the Owner and Creator of Talks with Maria (TwM), a Personal Development blog & podcast. Henderson is currently employed at a business coaching company, a mom to two and a wife.

Henderson writes on her spare time and is committed to further developing her knowledge in behavioral science, cognitive development and spiritual awareness to expand her writing catalog. The Boss Mom Mentality is a series of books, that create awareness, motivation and mindful approach to womanhood, A Book II to The Boss Mom Mentality is scheduled to be published in the Fall of 2020 and A Mindful Weightless Guide in the Summer of 2020.

To learn more, visit: www.talkswithmaria.com

Or Email Maria@talkswithmaria.com

"The future belongs to those who believe in the beauty of their dreams."

-Eleanor Roosevelt

Made in the USA
Monee, IL
05 December 2019